Care and Counselling Series

PEACE AT THE LAST

Other Books on Care and Counselling

Norman Autton

PEACE AT THE LAST
Talks with the Dying

FOREWORD BY
The Archbishop of Canterbury

LONDON
SPCK

First published 1978
SPCK
Holy Trinity Church
Marylebone Road
London NW1 4DU

Filmset in Great Britain by
Northumberland Press Ltd,
Gateshead, Tyne and Wear
and printed by
Richard Clay (The Chaucer Press) Ltd,
Bungay, Suffolk

ISBN 0 281 03575 X

O Lord, support us all the day long of this troublous life, until the shadows lengthen, and the evening comes, and the busy world is hushed, the fever of life is over, and our work is done. Then, Lord, in your mercy, grant us safe lodging, a holy rest, and peace at the last; through Jesus Christ our Lord.

John Henry Newman

A Court Jester was once called to the bedside of the King to beguile his sadness. The jester's mirth, however, failed for once. His best quips drew no corresponding smile from the king's pallid face. 'Master,' said the jester, 'why so sad?' 'Because', replied the king, 'I have to leave my home and people and go on a journey.' 'Is it a long journey?' asked the jester. 'It is indeed; the longest journey any man could take.' 'When are you going?' inquired the clown. 'I don't know for certain, but I think it will be quite soon, now.' 'But what of your majesty's preparations?' continued the jester. 'I see no clothing laid out, no boxes in the hall, no horses in the courtyard.' 'Alas!' was the reply, 'You speak the truth. I have had so much else to occupy me that I have made no preparations for departure.' 'Then take my cap and bells,' said the bold jester. 'I thought I was the court fool, but I see there lies here a greater fool than I, since he is going on the longest journey man ever took, and yet calls he me here to beguile his precious moments with jest and tale, instead of preparing for his travels.'

Contents

Acknowledgements

Thanks are due to the following for permission to quote from copyright sources:

William Collins Sons & Co. Ltd: *Journey for a Soul* by George Appleton; and *Miracle on the River Kwai* by Ernest Gordon

William B. Eerdmans Publishing Company: *Letters to an American Lady* by C. S. Lewis (used by permission)

The Guild of St Raphael: Form for the administration of Holy Unction

Harper & Row, Inc.: *Spiritual Counsels and Letters* by Baron von Hügel, edited by D. V. Steere

Alfred A. Knopf, Inc.: *The Plague* by Albert Camus © 1948 and translated by Stuart Gilbert: permission granted also by Hamish Hamilton Ltd, London; extract reprinted from *The Prophet* by Kahlil Gibran, with permission of the publisher, Alfred A. Knopf, Inc. Copyright 1923 by Kahlil Gibran; renewal copyright 1951 by Administrators C.T.A. of Kahlil Gibran Estate, and Mary G. Gibran

Longman Group Ltd: *The School of Charity* by Evelyn Underhill

Methodist Publishing House (Epworth Press): *Yonder: A Little Book for the Bereaved* by Leslie F. Church.

Extracts from the Book of Common Prayer and the Authorized Version of the Bible are Crown copyright and are reproduced with permission.

Extracts from the New English Bible, second edition copyright © 1970, are used by permission of Oxford and Cambridge University Presses.

Quotations from the Revised Standard Version of the Bible, copyrighted 1946 and 1952 by the Division of Christian Education of the National Council of the Churches of Christ in the U.S.A., are used by permission.

The source of the quotation on p. vii is unknown.

Foreword

I am very thankful that this book has been written. I believe it will be of real help to you as you read it, slowly, or as someone else reads it to you.

The writer is a man of God who has had long years of experience in various hospitals and has ministered to many hundreds of people in their illness. So he understands— and loves—and cares; and his book bears all the marks of that caring.

A great many fears will disappear as these chapters are read; and many readers will find that the peace of God, which passes all understanding, will keep their hearts and minds in Christ Jesus.

I pray that it may be so for you.

DONALD CANTUAR:

Lambeth Palace

Introduction

The past decade has seen much literature published on the subject of dying and death. Many of the books written have greatly helped to break the taboo with which our society masks the certainty and finality of death and have brought to light many valuable insights on the management of dying patients. Yet few if any of these recent publications set out to explain how best each of us can prepare for death.

We give due prominence and rightful emphasis to preparation for baptism and marriage, but very little if any for dying and death. We recognize that a vital part of education is to teach our children how to live; we seem unconcerned that no school curriculum includes instruction on how to die. Education for death is after all a very necessary preparation for a full and wholesome life. Indeed there seems to be no event in life for which we prepare so scantily as death. The Scottish poet, William Souter, left a day-to-day diary of his thoughts and feelings as he lay dying. In one extract he reveals that

> to know one is nearing the end of his life becomes a revelation of how dilatory one has been in the years when death seemed far away. My own days have been but loosely filled with accomplished tasks; in comfort and quiet, the tempo of one's living tends to become more and more easy-moving; the fulfilling of one's busyness more and more liable to be prolonged by the thought—'There is always tomorrow'. So much that I ought to have completed remains fragmentary or wholly unexpressed.
>
> *The Diaries of a Dying Man*

How wise therefore it is for us to see that our preparation is being taken seriously, our packing carefully arranged, and our journey prayerfully planned. The

wisdom of Pope John XXIII was evident when he re-
marked, on learning he was dying: 'My bags are packed,
I am ready to leave.' It is sad to reflect that most of us
make little or no provision for what is, after all, the
greatest event in life.

This book has been written to provide a simple and
straightforward guide free, it is hoped, from sentimen-
tality and unreality, to help us prepare for our departure.
It offers various routes by which we may possibly travel
and makes mention of some of the essential ingredients
we shall need for the journey. It takes the form of a series
of talks with the dying and deals with the importance of
facing up to the fact of death, the various fears which overcome us and how best they can be resolved. Some of the
psychological and emotional strains and stresses through
which we pass when our death becomes a reality are discussed. Information is given as to how best we can put
our affairs, both material and spiritual, in order, making
adequate provision for those we leave behind. The final
talks deal with the needs of young children, the bereaved
family, and the Christian hope of immortality.

Each talk has a specific theme which has been noted
in the heading. The material is meant to be used with
discretion and adjusted where necessary. It has been
assumed that the patient knows his or her condition. Where
he or she does not, it is still hoped that the talks will be
helpful. As much information as possible has been inserted
in the various talks so that those who read them can adapt
relevant passages from them rather than use them as they
stand. Each of us will, of course, differ in the words we
use and in the methods we adopt, but it is to be hoped
that some at least of the subjects mentioned and the
approaches outlined in the following pages will be of help
to all who are concerned in this most difficult and delicate
ministry. The talks are written primarily from the point
of view not of the priest or pastor, nor indeed of the
professional, but rather of all who have any share in the
care of the sick. For far too long have we left this

ministry to the professionals. Is it not time that the community as a whole realized its role and fulfilled its responsibility to the dying?

It is the humble and sincere prayer of the author that what has been written will serve to direct and guide those whose privilege it is to help and support the dying, in whatever capacity it may be. Where possible some of the talks may be read by the dying themselves: in many ways this is a book for Everyman, for all have to die. May it prompt each one of us to be more prepared and ready, so that when our time comes to set out on life's last and longest journey we may face the great unknown with hope, with courage and Christian joy.

NORMAN AUTTON
Epiphany 1977

TALK ONE
Facing the Facts

I understand that your doctor has been explaining to you the result of your operation and the various tests and X-rays you have had, and has intimated that your illness is rather a serious one. You may get over it but quite probably you may not. Although such news is distressing there is no need to abandon hope. Hope of improvement or of periods of remission should never be lost. Truth and hope are not mutually exclusive and this is no time for despair. You know the saying, 'Where there's life there's hope'. Well, it's equally true that 'Where there's hope there's life'. By hope I don't mean a sort of vague cheerfulness or wishful thinking. I mean a hope that's grounded on the assumption that whatever happens you are in God's hands. 'God's in his heaven, all's right with the world.' Try, if you can, to make some sense of your condition. Try to find some meaning in it all, however difficult that may be. Place it in God's hands and pray for God's grace to bear it and face it with patience and acceptance. Try to meet the challenge of it all as honestly as you can, however dark it may seem.

It is only natural for us to clutch at hope and associate it in our minds with getting well again or to reach out for 'miraculous cures'. Miracles of course do happen, and you must keep alive a will to live. This is very important. But realistic hope is facing up to the possibility of personal fulfilment in dying as well as in going on living. This is the hope that overcomes despair. In our seeking and searching for meaning and purpose and for assurance that we shall not be left alone or abandoned, we can gradually come to a new awareness of ourselves and our destiny, rather than giving ourselves up in despair and resigning ourselves to the inevitable. If therefore you yourself can come to accept death as the natural fulfilment of life and

5

the completion of its meaning and purpose, you will be able to face up to things with a sense of fulfilment and find much peace and tranquillity not only for yourself but for all those about you. Julian of Norwich once put it like this: 'God wills that ... we be ever strong in sure trust, in weal and woe, for he loves and likes us, and so wills He that we love and like Him, and mightily trust in Him, and all shall be well.'

You have probably been suspicious about your symptoms for some little time. We all are far more knowledgeable these days about our various ailments and complaints, and of course when we are confined to bed we have plenty of time to think about our aches and pains. You may have felt over the past weeks that you have not been improving as much as you had hoped. Other patients on the ward have come and gone, and here you are still in bed. Perhaps up until now you have been struggling against acknowledging the real facts of your illness, even to yourself, and been determined to conceal your innermost feelings from those near and dear to you. Now that the doctor has told you the truth you can at least adjust more easily to the situation.

I'm sure you would agree that it's much better to know the truth than to be tossed to and fro in uncertainty with different people telling you different things. This would only have left you more and more bewildered and confused. You would not have known who was telling you the true facts about your condition. Now you know where you stand. I shall always remember a young patient saying to me after the doctor had broken the news to her that she would probably not recover from her illness: 'You may think it strange but in some mysterious way my life is far fuller and richer now that I know the truth. It was a shock when I first heard the news, but instead of being ninety per cent depressed and ten per cent happy, as I was before, I'm now ninety per cent happy and ten per cent depressed.' I know we all react to things differently but I'm sure her feelings are shared by many other patients in like condition.

When we are very ill and have to face up to the crisis of a serious illness with all its possible consequences, what we need most, apart from relief of pain, is to share our feelings, our anxieties and hopes with someone with whom we can talk, calmly and unemotionally. This is one of the reasons why I'm pleased to have this opportunity of talking with you, for we can now be open and frank with each other. We meet sickness best when we sense we are accepted and understood just as we are, and that we shall not be alone when we face whatever may be before us.

One of the first things you should try to do is to face up to the reality of your condition. In serious illness death must always be seen as a possible outcome, and it is wise to make provisions for it. Just think for a moment what it would be like if there was no death; if we all went on living for ever and ever as we are now. What a dreadful prospect that would be! It's an appalling thought, isn't it? Of one thing we are all certain—that is that we all have to die. For some death may be a long way off; for others it may be near. Perhaps you have already been thinking about this. To prepare for death is the highest duty and the greatest privilege of the Christian. How wise therefore it is for each of us to see that our preparation is being taken seriously, our packing carefully arranged, and our journey prayerfully planned for what after all is going to be the greatest event of our life. The art of living well and the art of dying well are both one.

There is the tendency these days to deny the fact of death—to shut it out of our minds. You've probably noticed how we all have a habit of avoiding the use of the very word 'death'. We talk of people 'passing on' or 'passing away'. There are some people who seem to think that all we need is more and more progress in medical research and a cure will eventually be found for every disease and disorder. We shall then reach the stage of never having to die at all! But death is normal. It's as normal as birth, and the universal experience of death is all too plain to dismiss its one solemn certainty from our minds. Each one of us has to die! Oh yes, we may shrink from it; we may want to be sheltered from all thought of it; we may dislike talking about it; we may resolve to play games of 'make-believe'; but escape it we can never. Try as we may to forget, the fact of death cannot be forgotten; deny it as we may, death itself remains undeniable. Any of us may die at any time; all of us must die sometime. The circumstances which will surround our deaths, the manner of our dying, the time of our dying, the scene of our dying, are for all of us uncertain and unpredictable, but the fact that we shall all die is absolutely certain.

You may be thinking that such ideas as these only tend to make you feel gloomy and morbid. But preparation for the coming of death need not depress you at all. Indeed the very opposite is true; in many ways your life can now become more full, more fruitful, more mature than perhaps ever before. This can become for you, if you will, a time of deeper awareness of spiritual realities. It can be a challenge which can bring out the best in you—a time of receiving and giving, of meaning and of joy. It is not those who think about death and prepare for it who are most in bondage to its fears and threats. No! it is rather those who've been determined to put such thoughts on one side and to neglect all preparation for it who are most frightened and depressed when their time comes.

The very uncertainty of the time and manner of our death, so mercifully and lovingly hidden from us, should make us want to prepare, to do our best while we may. If only we could be certain in our prediction about the hour of our death there might be something to be said for postponing our preparation, or putting aside until later all serious thoughts about it. But because of its very uncertainty there is surely no greater folly than to hide ourselves from its grim pursuit.

What you and I have to remember is that we've only a lease and not a freehold of this earthly life of ours. If you can only have the courage to confront death openly and honestly, without any attempt at evasion or deceit, you will find eventually that much of its sting will be lost for you. There will be less and less difficulty about the possibility of dying, and death in itself will become more acceptable. You will be able to move towards it, as it were, seeing it not as an unknown enemy but as a welcome friend.

Now this does not mean of course that you have to dwell upon death continuously in a morbid sort of way. There is a saying which is so true: 'We cannot look at the sun all the time: neither can we look at death all the time.' From time to time you may need to resort to a little make-believe, for not all of us can face death like a St Francis of Assisi, who, on hearing he had not long to live, 'spread out his hands to the Lord with very great devotion and reverence, and said with great joy of mind and body, "Welcome, Sister Death".' To some of us, perhaps including yourself, our Lord sometimes says: 'There is still much that I could say to you, but the burden would be too great for you now' (John 16.12). Death is never easy to accept.

Perhaps you have been thinking that death is something that is going to happen to 'the other person'. One of the major adjustments you may now have to make is to recognize the fact that it is quite possibly happening to *you*. If you are prepared to be open and honest and express some of your feelings, then in our forthcoming talks together we can deal with each situation as it arises and take it step by step as it comes.

You will appreciate, I know, that there can be no pre-conceived or stereotyped reactions to the approach of death. Much will depend upon our personal conflicts and needs, our individual life-style, age, our values and relationships. Death itself will mean different things to each one of us, for death is personal and responses to it are exceedingly personal.

In this initial talk we have been able at least to be honest and frank with each other. We have seen how essential it is to be prepared for death whenever it may come. I am pleased we have been able to discuss some of the things which were obviously on your mind and which you have been finding it difficult to bring out into the open. Perhaps you would like to think about them further, and we can have another talk later on.

Meanwhile, 'may the God of hope fill you with all joy and peace by your faith in him, until, by the power of the Holy Spirit, your whole life and outlook is radiant with hope' (Rom. 15.13).

TALK TWO
Your Thoughts

When you were first told the full truth about the seriousness of your illness and its likely outcome, you were naturally very shocked. You just could not believe it. You were angry, bitter, and resentful. 'Why should this be happening to me?' was the way you put it. 'What have I done to deserve this?' you asked. 'Surely the diagnosis can't be right. They've probably mixed up the X-rays. No! It can't be true—it just isn't true!' you protested. As the days have gone by and you have had a chance to reflect and to talk things over, you seem to be working through some of these very natural and normal reactions.

In this present talk together I would like, if I may, to explain to you very simply how some of these reactions arise, and how these feelings of denial, anger, and depression affect us. It's only by talking about them openly and understanding how they work that we are able to face them and eventually overcome them.

Now one of the most common reactions to being told 'bad news' is that of denial. We naturally protest—'It can't be true!' We simply don't want to hear news of this kind, so we forget or suppress it. We want to pretend, not only to our family and friends but even to ourselves, that we are not as seriously ill as we really are. The doctor may have gone out of his way to tell us as plainly as he could about our condition, but we don't take it in because we just don't want to hear it. And because we have not 'heard' it, we give vent to such remarks as: 'Doctors don't tell you a thing! No one explains anything to you when you're in hospital.' We are inclined to block and shut out anything unpleasant in the same way as we close our eyes if anything offends our sight, or we turn aside or move away from anything that is distasteful to us. These are some of the unconscious mechanisms which we constantly use in our everyday lives, even when we are fit and well. The purpose of denial is to enable us to cope with the threat of any impending danger or potential calamity.

From time to time you will probably find yourself denying the true facts of your illness or its diagnosis and prognosis, in spite of what the doctor has told you. These periods of denial are often most necessary, particularly if they can serve to strengthen hope and prevent despair.

As I have already said, it would be well-nigh impossible to live our lives without being able at times to deny or negate certain aspects of our everyday experiences. So your response of denial—'It's not me!'—is quite a healthy and normal response to shock. It gives you a breathing space to prepare and strengthen your inner resources which otherwise might prove too much for you to bear. It enables you to look at a small piece of your problem at a time, and once you have faced up to this, you will then feel the more able to work realistically at a little bit more. Partial denial of this kind can therefore be beneficial. It is when denial becomes prolonged that you are likely to find yourself in difficulties, for it can then prevent you from facing up to the reality of your illness. It can interfere and inhibit your relationship with those around you. A long period of denial can prompt you to put off further treatment. Try whenever possible to shade your periods of denial into moods of optimism and you will find that they then serve as healthy attitudes, for feelings of hope and confidence are very necessary for you at the present time. They make it possible for you to gather up sufficient resource to face your present illness. They give you zest and encourage a will to live. If you have someone to talk to about the real issues of your illness, you will find you will be more able to work through these phases of denial. I hope these talks together are enabling you to do just that.

What about when we are angry and bitter? When we are ill we can direct these feelings against anyone—God, the Church, the hospital, the doctors, or even those who are looking after us. Do not be alarmed if you find yourself questioning your belief in God or being angry with him sometimes. I know you felt at one stage that he was punishing you, and you were very resentful. You said you had always lived a good life, kept up your prayers, and gone to church regularly. What sort of a God was he to do this to you? you wanted to know. All very natural reactions, and if handled aright they can have a positive outcome. Anger is an instinctive emotion, part of our natural endowment. The psalmists for example were never afraid to tell God exactly how they felt. They simply and frankly poured out their fears, their anger, and their sorrows to him. 'When my heart is vexed', they said, 'I will complain!' Whenever you feel angry talk frankly with someone about it and get it out of your system. If your feelings of envy and bitterness do not find an outlet they will only turn inwards upon yourself. Do try then as often as you can to bring them out into the open and let the steam out of them, as it were. I am pretty certain that those who are near and dear to you will understand. If you are still unhappy about this and think that what you say will hurt or criticize your loved ones in any way, you need never be afraid to tell God about your feelings. He can take them even if others cannot. Tell him exactly how you feel, offering him the whole of your being in utter honesty and frankness.

You know how much better we all feel when we are able to speak to someone who has been through all that we are having to suffer at present—someone, for example, who is able to say, 'I know exactly how you are feeling for I, too, have suffered as you are suffering now.' Well, there is someone to whom you can take these feelings, 'for since he himself has passed through the test of suffering, he is able to help those who are meeting their test now' (Heb. 2.18). Indeed you will sometimes find that such open expression of feelings will tend to ease some of your physical pain and distress, as well as help to calm you emotionally and bring you peace of mind.

You've been telling me how depressed you've been these last few days. When moods of this kind afflict us, as they often do in illness, there's the tendency to look back and judge ourselves, often harshly, wishing we had lived a better life and regretting much that has happened in the past. We realize that there has been so much left undone. When we have these moods we seem to magnify our faults and failings, and exaggerate our feelings of unworthiness. We feel that life has been unfair to us and become despondent at the thought of being more and more dependent on those around us. All these inhibitions become a threat to our meaning and significance as a person. I am glad however that you are now able to speak frankly and honestly to me about them. Never be ashamed to share them. Jesus on his cross cried out in utter depression, 'My God, my God, why have you deserted me?' It is he and he alone who can say to you, 'I am with you in the depths of your despair, for I know what it is to have passed through the valley of the shadow.' When things seem at their worst, when life is darkest, always remember God is still master of the situation and he will see you through. You will never have to suffer alone. Behind all your depression and gloom there is a God who not only cares but shares. No longer will your suffering and depression be a predicament when you recognize God through his Holy Spirit immanent in your life and present in your pain.

Having that good cry probably did you a power of good! Do you feel better now? Unfortunately we sometimes think it unmanly and childish to cry. Please don't apologize or feel ashamed. Remember, it is always better to cry outwardly than inwardly. Someone once said 'It takes a man to cry!', and so it does. Whenever you feel like crying have a good cry. It's something we all feel like doing at times, particularly when we are weak and in low spirits and things seem to be going against us. It is surprising how much better and brighter we feel afterwards. When we give vent to our feelings there's always a great sense of relief.

14

When we feel low and depressed an intensity of guilt and shame often makes us convinced that we are only getting what we deserve. Don't ever think of your illness as a punishment for sins you may have committed in the past. God does not send suffering either to 'punish us', or 'to make us good'. He does however allow suffering in the world as he allows sin to exist. You and I are members of the whole human family in its estrangement from God, who is the source of our life and health, and we all share in the corporate sin of the world. We can go on asking 'why?', but there is no complete answer to the problem of suffering. In this life our understanding can only be partial and provisional. Here 'we see only puzzling reflections in a mirror' (1 Cor. 13.12), as St Paul puts it. It is only natural to ask 'why?', but I'm sure you'll find it more helpful to ask 'what?'—'What is God saying to me during this time of sickness?' or 'how?'—'How can I bring something positive out of this situation?' More than anyone he might, with full justification, have asked 'why?' All these different reactions I have tried to explain to you— shock, denial, anger, depression—are but natural and you will find that your attitudes and moods are quite likely to vary from day to day, even from moment to moment. What you are able to bear today, you may want to shun tomorrow; courage and despair, optimism and pessimism all seem to alternate and interact. I'm afraid there are no easy or straightforward answers to the problems and diffi- culties we've been talking about. The problem of suffering is a very real one and much still remains in the realm of the unknown, inexplicable by any human understanding. What we have to do is to try to discover a providential pattern in it all rather than see it as totally meaningless and wasteful; to see somehow, through the darkness of suffering, the lights of a loving purpose. Rather than puzzle your head about it all there is something far better you can do. You can take hold of the hand of Christ and walk through it, for it is only through him that you can learn to find and face the true meaning of your present suffering.

We can never hope to understand it or bear it on our own. 'Lord, I believe: help my unbelief.'

Christ allows you to suffer, but I can assure you that he will never let you suffer more than you can bear. 'God keeps faith, and he will not allow you to be tested above your powers, but when the test comes he will at the same time provide a way out, by enabling you to sustain it' (1 Cor. 10.13). This doesn't mean that you have to submit meekly to your suffering. Such submission can only be passive and negative. Neither does it imply that you have to resign yourself stoically to it. What you have to do is to try to accept it as your share in the tragedy of life; to take up your suffering and challenge it. This is the attitude which is active and positive. It is not suffering in itself which ennobles us but rather the way we face up to it and bear it. Our response to suffering is the all-important factor. When St Paul had 'a sharp pain' in his body he prayed about it and then recognized that the answer and help from God came not in its removal but in the strength given him to see it through. He was given an inner staying power to face up to things. Suffering is always a crucial test of our courage and our faith.

Consecrated suffering is creative; it is indeed a form of action even though you are at present lying in a sick-bed. It is a medium in which Christ can work; it is material with which his Spirit can create that which is good and that which will last. Then a final thought—in such suffering, accepted, offered, you do find the living Christ, who himself endured the cross, quite remarkably near. He says to you, as he said of old to his disciples when they were frightened and fearful: 'It is I, be not afraid.' When you are certain of that blessed companionship you can then put up with anything. You can be sure, even though faith goes blindfold, that 'all things work together for good to them that love God'. Whenever you feel burdened or overcome, listen for that word from him—'It is I, be not afraid.'

Christ said not:

> 'Thou shalt not be tempested;
> Thou shalt not be travailed;
> Thou shalt not be afflicted.'

But he said, 'Thou shalt not be overcome.'

(Julian of Norwich)

TALK THREE
Your Fears

I hope your doctor will explain to you, as far as he is able, what course your illness is likely to take. Do feel perfectly free to ask him any questions, and if there is anything worrying you, do not hesitate to tell him. For example, you may want to know if you will have to stay in hospital long, or whether there's any likelihood of your being able to go home soon. The fear of pain and the possibility of having to undergo another operation were, I know, very much on your mind. Many of these worrying thoughts can be relieved by having a talk with your doctor when next he comes around. After all it's only he who is in a position to give you the full facts about your illness and put your mind at ease. Fears and fantasies about what is likely to happen to you as your illness progresses are very natural, and unless you approach your doctor he will not be aware that you are worried.

You asked me the other day how best you could deal with some of your fears, and I promised to suggest some thoughts which may possibly help you work through some of them. As you can well appreciate, the fear of death is a very complex subject, and it has all sorts of conscious and unconscious aspects. The first thing to remember is that such fear is both normal and natural. The dread of death is an instinct which is common to all of us. John Bunyan in his *Pilgrim's Progress* tells us that Christian, for all his fervent desire to reach the Celestial City, is stunned by 'a great darkness and horror' when he attempts to cross the river, 'so that he could neither remember nor orderly talk of any of those sweet refreshments that he had met with in the way of his pilgrimage'.

If you are feeling at all frightened at this time take comfort from the fact that Jesus himself became anxious as his death drew near. It may help you if I read to you some

18

passages from the Passion story. In the garden of Gethsemane 'horror and dismay came over him, and he said to them, "My heart is ready to break with grief"' (Mark 14.34). Such was his anguish that 'his sweat was like clots of blood falling to the ground' (Luke 22.44). As he viewed his death he was 'troubled in spirit' and was ready to confess, 'I have a baptism to undergo, and how hampered I am until the ordeal is over' (Luke 12.50). On the cross Jesus himself cried out, 'My God, my God, why hast thou forsaken me?' So don't ever be ashamed at feeling afraid. After all, it's only human to fear death.

When these fears of death come into your mind—and we all have them from time to time—it does not always mean that you haven't sufficient faith. Personal sanctity is no talisman against fears such as these. Faith is being prepared to confess your fears, bringing them out into the open and asking for strength to see you through. It's always better to express your feelings honestly, as you are doing at present, and to look them in the face than to suppress and fight against them. It's the worst thing possible to pretend they are not there, and to try and live in a world of make-believe. 'Though I am sometimes afraid yet put I my trust in thee', said the Psalmist, and you may like to repeat those words of his to yourself when you are feeling anxious or frightened. 'Though ... I ... am ... sometimes ... afraid ... yet ... put ... I ... my ... trust ... in ... thee.'

You have, I know, been thinking of the future, and what you may have to face. One of the difficulties is that dying is strange and unknown to us, for we have never done it before. Not one of us has had the experience of death. No one has ever come back to tell us what actually happens when death occurs and what lies on 'the other side'.

> Strange, is it not? that of the myriads who
> Before us passed the door of Darkness through,
> Not one returns to tell us of the Road,
> Which to discover we must travel too.

The Rubáiyát of Omar Khayyam, tr. Edward Fitzgerald

We all love the familiar and we instinctively fear and shun the strange. What the unknown has in store for each one of us is beyond not only our experience but also our imagination. I remember one patient who had been hovering between life and death describing her experience in rather vivid terms. 'So I lay upon the edge of death looking out,' she said. 'It lay just there—that great beyond—and I saw it as one sees the earth at sunrise from the window of a tower; yet how it was is difficult to tell, for the things outside of this world are outside of this world's speech.'

You may sometimes fear that you will be gradually cut off from yourself and from those about you. Visits from friends may appear to be less frequent and conversation can become somewhat strained at times. The impact of all this is an increasing sense of isolation. You may possibly have fears of being abandoned and unloved. Loneliness is one of the most dreadful and fearful of all experiences, and death is something no one else can do for us. No one else can enter into that tremendous experience which awaits us all. You may sometimes feel that the doctor or nurse who used to call in to your room or sit by your bedside no longer seems to have time to stay. People can appear to be in a hurry, and even your best friends seem sometimes lost for words. We meet sickness best when we sense we are being accepted and understood just as we are, and that we shall not be alone when we face whatever may be before us. The staff here will see that you are not alone and will care and support you at all times. With love they can create a warm atmosphere of caring in which you can just be yourself, express yourself freely, for you will know that your integrity and individuality as a person is being respected and maintained. Such an assurance will help you to come to terms with both your illness and yourself.

I'm sure you must wondering what will happen to your family and your dependants after your days. We naturally dread being taken away from those we love. Death disrupts our union with the world and with our nearest and dearest. It is hard to say good-bye to those we love. I remember someone who had undergone a series of operations for cancer and knew that he did not have very long to live; he put it like this. He felt we reach a stage when we pass beyond the need of human love and begin to experience a deeper relationship with Love himself—a love which can in itself be totally satisfying. 'I believe the time will come', he said, 'when we experience a greater need which will only be satisfied by Love himself, namely God. Love which will place all our other loves in their true perspective; Love which will include all our friendships and relationships, and make sense of them for all time, and yet also enrich them for all time. "Gather up the fragments that remain, that nothing be lost", said Jesus. God never takes away what we have been given. He gathers it all up and makes of the fragments of our human loves a whole, an entirety limitless in wonder and glory.'

As well as the fear *of* leaving loved ones behind, there is also fear *for* those who are being left behind. I wonder if you've been thinking how the family will manage and who will look after the children. One of the ways in which you can ensure that they will be well cared for and looked after is to make every provision for this now and to see that the necessary arrangements for their welfare have been discussed with family and friends. This is something that I hope to talk to you about later.

As your sickness progresses it's possible you may need to become more and more dependent on others. Should you at any time become incontinent this may evoke in you a sense of shame, or a feeling of resentment, particularly if you happen to be a rather sensitive person. But doctors and nurses are well used to patients being in this state so please do not feel too embarrassed. The nursing staff are looking after a number of patients in similar circumstances every day on the wards. Please remember, too, that you yourself can do much to help them by being cooperative and responsive to treatment. Think of yourself more as an agent than as a patient.

If you should have any discomfort, pain, vomiting, or symptoms of breathlessness, do be assured that much can be done to relieve these symptoms, and the doctors and nurses will be helping you all they can. Whatever happens they will see you through, offering you their understanding and knowledge and giving you every possible relief for your suffering and pain. Sometimes you may feel that your hold on life is being gradually lessened; you want to be active but are forced to be passive. You want to change your circumstances but you cannot. All these are natural but irritating and frustrating effects of being ill.

The dread of pain has been worrying you quite a lot, I know. The thought of physical pain can make you anxious and frightened, but you'll find that the more fearful you become the greater your sensitivity to pain. It may make you angry and resentful, irritable and full of self-pity. Often *mental* pain becomes more difficult to bear than physical pain—for example, the depression that comes with sickness, or the feelings of guilt over what we have left undone. Pain, whether physical or mental, can lead to an excessive preoccupation with self. It makes you lose interest in other people and in things around.

Fortunately, as I've said, much can be done these days to relieve pain and physical discomfort. Pain can now be regularly controlled and this means that you can be kept pain-free and alert instead of being left drugged and comatose, as used to be the case before all these new drugs were introduced. When we are very ill we sometimes have a fear of judgement and thoughts of punishment torment us. Almost instinctively we associate the thought of death with feelings of guilt. There can also be genuine feelings of dissatisfaction with what we've made of our lives. As death comes nearer our sense of guilt seems to grow in intensity. There is a tendency for us to look back over the past and recall opportunities which have been neglected and privileges we have misused.

22

One of the best ways to calm your fears is to bring them out into the open. You should never be ashamed or apologetic about having any of these fears I've been describing. We all have fears of varying kinds. We wouldn't be human if we didn't. Many people try to steel themselves against them and do their best to resist them. This only serves to sap more and more energy and leaves the way open to further weakness, depression, and weariness. It is far better to face them and share them with someone you can really trust, someone who has a sympathetic and understanding ear. What about talking for example to your doctor or your ward sister, the nurse who looks after you, the hospital chaplain, the social worker, or a member of your family—anyone with whom you've been able to form a close and intimate relationship: someone with whom you can talk freely and honestly. Such companionship will help you face up to your worries and I'm sure you will be given a great deal of strength and comfort as a result.

We are all so very different and no one person's reactions to a serious illness are the same as another's. For instance if we happen to be elderly and have been in pain and discomfort for some time we shall probably see death as a release and a peaceful end to our labours. If we are young or middle-aged we are inclined to rebel against the very fact of death and become very much aware of unfinished tasks and unfulfilled ideals and aspirations. What I would like you to bear in mind is that the process of dying is normally gradual and gentle. It seems comparable to falling asleep. The stage which precedes death may possibly be painful but dying in itself is not. Indeed many would say that the fear of death can be more painful than the process of dying itself. Again fear can be far more acute and overwhelming for our family and our friends than it is for ourselves. In the majority of instances a calm serenity and a quiet phase of surrender help us to accept the inevitable. In the majority of instances there comes a blissful feeling of complete resignation when we look forward to release from pain and suffering, especially if we have

23

had a particularly difficult and painful illness. When the end is near there always seems a perfect willingness to die, and we rarely experience the fears which may have been with us earlier. When the hour of our death is upon us fear is almost invariably stilled and we usually face the end with a peaceful and serene mind.

I recently came across a prayer about the fear of dying, which I want to share with you. It can serve as a fitting conclusion to this present talk together.

Lord, I love you very much and really do want to be with you always, but I am afraid of dying. Give me the kind of faith in you that will not waver, the kind of hope which will help me to believe that you will be with me even to the end of the world, and the kind of love that will trust you completely whatever happens. Keep me in peace and guard me from fear, for the sake of your dear Son who knows human frailty so well.

The Shade of His Hand, Michael Hollings and Etta Gullick

How to Deal with Them 1

I promised to do my best to help you deal with some of the apprehensions and fears that are worrying and disturbing you. 'How does one kill fear, I wonder?' asks Joseph Conrad in his novel *Lord Jim*. 'How do you shoot a spectre through the heart, slash off its spectral head, take it by its spectral throat?' I want to try to suggest at least some weapons which may stave off its attacks. One of the main instruments I can thoroughly recommend is prayer, for prayer is the great conquering force against fear. I don't mean long strainful efforts to pray. No, just quiet moments of calm and relaxation. When we're ill our energy gets quickly sapped up and we seem to suffer from a sort of spiritual inertia. All this of course in turn has an effect upon our prayer life, but once you start praying I'm sure you'll soon find that it is God who will do most of the work for you.

You've already been meeting some of the practical difficulties about saying your prayers in a busy ward. There's the lack of privacy, constant noise, and frequent interruptions. In these circumstances don't worry if you can't pray in words. God isn't really concerned about your words —what he wants is your heart. *Think* your prayers rather than *say* them. I mean by this to rest upon the love of God and do nothing which will entail any effort, physical, mental, or spiritual. Prayer can be 'contemplative in-action'. Offer yourself up to God as far as you're able, for 'prayer is the soul's desire, uttered or unexpressed'. Your thoughts can be your prayers, and whatever your position in bed 'your soul can be on its knees'. Your suffering can pray and your patience can be an unspoken prayer. Even your wish to pray can be a most valuable prayer in itself. A saintly bishop (Jeremy Taylor) used to say: 'We may pray in bed, everywhere and at all times and in all circumstances and it is well if we do so.'

It will be enough to know that you are with him and he with you. 'Father here am I, and here are you.' Just relax a little and get quite still within yourself, and try to face your problems. You'll then be able to rest upon God's strength. St Paul puts it like this: 'The Lord is near; have no anxiety, but in everything make your requests known to God in prayer and petition with thanksgiving. Then the peace of God, which is beyond our utmost understanding, will keep guard over your hearts and your thoughts, in Christ Jesus' (Phil. 4.6–7).

In your prayers try simply to tell God exactly how you're feeling. For example you can say, 'O God, I'm very frightened, please help me to be less afraid', or 'Give me the courage to face whatever may be before me'. You can tell him: 'There are so many things I don't understand at present, help me just to abide in your presence, and leave all in your hands.' These short sentences—they're sometimes known as 'arrowhead' prayers—will help you cast out your fears and serve to intersperse thoughts of God during any periods of doubt and apprehension you may have. You'll find they'll prove especially beneficial in times of temptation, during spasms of pain, or when you lie awake at night. Here are some other suggestions which I shall leave with you. You can adapt them for each particular need:

Though I am sometimes afraid yet put I my trust in thee.

Father, into thy hands I commit my spirit.

Help me to bear my pain and to suffer for you.

O Lord, by your cross and passion, strengthen me.

I will fear no evil for thou art with me.

O Lord, in you have I trusted, let me never be confounded.

Our help is in the name of the Lord.

Your will be done.

The Lord is my light and my salvation: who should I fear?

Be still and know that I am God.

Be assured, I am with you always, to the end of time.

These short yet strong expressions of faith can be used at any time, and you can repeat them slowly at intervals over and over again. When I was reading to you from the Passion story in the Gospels the other afternoon you probably remember how Jesus himself in the garden of Gethsemane prayed 'using the same words as before'. Throughout the whole night he prayed, 'Thy will be done'. Don't worry if you fall asleep when you're praying. Prayer can be continued in your unconscious mind.

When the ward is quiet and you're on your own you can close your eyes and try to picture our Lord on his cross and offer him yourself and your sufferings. As I've told you before, don't be afraid to take your fears, even your anger and resentment to him, should you sometimes feel embittered or 'hard done by'. I wonder, have you ever read those delightful little stories about Don Camillo, the honest village priest and his deadly opponent, the communist mayor? Don Camillo shares his real feelings with Christ and is never afraid to tell him what he really thinks. You, too, can bring him your innermost thoughts and worries and lay them before him. Let your prayer be a personal conversation with God. Just be yourself and begin where you are and tell him how things are. You haven't to feel 'good' or 'holy', but you have to be honest. In any case it's a sheer waste of time trying to hide anything from God. He already knows how you are feeling, for he is the God 'unto whom all hearts are open, all desires known, and from whom no secrets are hid'. Christ knows exactly how you're feeling and understands the difficulties you're facing.

Another method which I'm sure you'll find reassuring is the use of daily acts of faith, charity, repentance, resignation, and surrender. Throughout the day you can repeat such phrases as: 'Thy will be done *in* me, *through* me, *by* me, and *to* me this day'; 'Jesus is with me. Jesus is in me'. These 'affirmations', as they are called, will help to strengthen you to face and overcome moments of gloom and depression. They'll enable you to realize Christ's presence more and more, so that you won't feel alone in your pain and suffering. You'll come to learn that he suffers not only in you and through you but with you.

You may feel happier using your own words rather than set prayers, for by using your own words you will thereby be making your prayers personal. If you do, it's always helpful to end your prayers on a note of confidence —e.g., 'I will bless the Lord at all times: his praise shall continually be in my mouth' (Ps. 34.1). Or 'Be merciful unto me, O God, be merciful unto me: For my soul trusteth in thee: yea, in the shadow of thy wings will I make my refuge, until these calamities be overpast' (Ps. 57.1).

Don't worry too much about the details of your prayers. Just pray 'as you can and not as you can't'. The fewer the words the better. Our Lord's actual words of prayer in the garden of Gethsemane were very few and short, yet they seem to have said everything that was necessary. Just rely as firmly as you can upon the prayers of the Church on earth and in heaven and rest in the Lord. Relax in the presence of Christ, for he may be saying to you, as he said to Martha, 'You are fretting and fussing about so many things; but one thing is necessary. The part that Mary has chosen is best' (Luke 10.41–2)—seating herself at his feet and staying there listening to his words.

If you feel up to it sometimes, especially in moments of loneliness or self-pity, why not make use of the opportunities you have for the practice of intercessory prayer. You can begin by praying for those around you in the ward. Let yourself be filled with the love of God—for them. Look not only at Christ but with Christ—look at the people around you as he would look at them, and see them as he sees them. You can sympathize with them now with a greater degree of intimacy than when you were well. If this is too much of a mental or physical strain for you select just one particular person by name for special intercession. Our Lord did this for St Peter, you may remember: 'Simon, Simon, take heed: Satan has been given leave to sift all of you like wheat; but for you I have prayed that your faith may not fail' (Luke 22.31–2). You can pray for one person without necessarily praying less for others. Suffering adds effectiveness to our intercessory prayers. It lends power to our prayers, bringing to him the pains and sorrows of all men. I hope that you'll find that such thoughts as these will help you to forget some of your own troubles and dispel many of your fears.

How to Deal with Them 2

I know that in the past few days you've been in a lot of pain and discomfort and are naturally dreading the thought of more pain. To be in pain must be very wearisome and hard to bear. Don't hesitate to make use of the pain-relieving drugs which the doctor prescribes for you. Never think you have to bear unnecessary pain. There's a very real place for drugs in painful illness, for after all they're God-given and are to be received with much thankfulness and prayer. We can never cease to be grateful for morphia and other pain-killing drugs. The Christian attitude towards pain is to avoid it, but not at all costs. Sometimes it is necessary to meet it and challenge it with courage and gratitude. I know nothing about the medical or pharmaceutical details of the various drugs you're taking, but what I can do is to pass on to you some thoughts which I hope will help you during periods of pain.

Each of us in varying degrees has to share in the pain of the world; for some the burden is light while for others it is heavy. We can't choose but we can accept it, and whatever your own particular share happens to be, always remember that you are at no time suffering alone but always *with* and *in* Christ. As a member of Christ you're sharing in 'the fellowship of the sufferings of Christ' and contributing blessings to others, to 'his Body the Church'. In a mysterious but very real way you're helping to fill up what is left over of the sufferings of Christ.

This doesn't mean to say, of course, that the pain won't still be painful. I don't want to give you the impression that I'm glorifying pain or conferring a sort of morbid mystique on suffering. Pain doesn't cease to be pain. What happens is that it no longer becomes purposeless. You'll be able in other words to bring something out of your pain, and when you realize that pain need never be useless or futile but can be turned into a blessing, you'll somehow find a new strength to bear it. Pain seems to link you more and more closely to others in the fellowship of suffering. It creates sympathy with those about you and brings out the best in them. Seeing how you bear your pain gives them added courage and renewed cheerfulness. A feature of pain is that it can be shared. We belong to each other and have the pain and joy of feeling and sharing the needs of one another. There is no such thing as a separate person, for we are united with all men in the family of pain. We can never live as isolated individuals. In your pain you are taking your share in the world's pain, for pain brings us into communion and fellowship with all who suffer. It can give us a power to help others greater than anything we may have possessed when we were fit and well. Someone who had spent years in and out of hospital and had been in considerable pain once told his friends that

> in entrusting us with a load of pain God is often giving us a power to help others greater than that possessed by the most eloquent of preachers or the wisest of teachers. To carry with us that which automatically brings out the best side of other people, that which sends them away with fresh courage and renewed cheerfulness, that which brings them nearer to each other, and to goodness, and therefore to God, what more lovely ministry could any of us desire?
>
> *A Parson's Thoughts on Pain*, G. E. Childs

I can do no better than leave with you some practical thoughts about how we can face up to pain. They are words which were written by a very saintly person, and they have helped countless others in moments of pain and discomfort.

> Try more and more at the moment itself, without any delay or evasion, without any fixed form, as simply, as spontaneously as possible, to cry out to God, to Christ

31

our Lord, in any way that comes most handy, and the more variously the better ... 'Oh, may this pang deepen me, may it help to make me real, real—really humble, really loving, really ready to live or die with my soul in Thy hands' ... And so on, and so on. You could end by such ejaculations costing your brain practically nothing. The all-important point is, to make them at the time and with the pain well mixed up into the prayer.

Spiritual Counsels and Letters, Baron von Hügel

Pain can enable us to see more deeply not only into ourselves but also into other people. It forces us to look at life from a different angle, often from a higher plane. There are some truths which can only be seen through tear-stained eyes. Try if you possibly can to serve God in and through your pain. Pray the Gethsemane prayer of Jesus—'Lord, if it be possible, let this cup pass from me; nevertheless not as I will but as thou wilt' (Matt. 26.39)—that you may be granted the power and the discernment to do the will of God.

Another effective antidote to fear is hope. Try to share all you can in St Paul's conviction that 'there is nothing in death or life, in the realm of spirits or superhuman powers, in the world as it is or the world as it shall be, in the forces of the universe, in heights or depths—nothing in all creation that can separate us from the love of God in Christ Jesus our Lord' (Rom. 8.38–9). We do not know the future, but we do know the God of the future, 'Jesus Christ, the same yesterday, today and for ever.' What he has been to us in the past, what he is in the present, that we may be sure he will be to us in the future. There's a sixteenth-century prayer which runs, 'Let come what will come, God's will is well come.'

I wonder if you're familiar with the Third Collect for Morning Prayer? I'll read it to you slowly: 'O Lord, our heavenly Father, almighty and everlasting God, who has safely brought us to the beginning of *this day*: defend us in the same with thy mighty power; and grant that *this day* we fall into no sin, neither run into any kind of danger; but that all our doings may be ordered by thy governance, to do always that which is righteous in thy sight: through Jesus Christ our Lord.' As you see it teaches us to live our lives just a day at a time, not tripping over each day because of our anxieties for the morrow. If you try to do this much of your fear of the future will be resolved. Jesus said, 'Do not be anxious about tomorrow; tomorrow will look after itself. Each day has troubles enough of its own' (Matt. 6.34). Today, and tomorrow, may end very differently from what you *hope*. Yes, but they may end very differently from what you *fear*. Each day brings its problems and difficulties but each day brings fresh supplies of grace to meet them. We pray, 'Give us *this* day our daily bread', not for tomorrow and the next day but for 'this day'. 'Lord, for tomorrow and its needs I do not pray, just for today.' So often our trust is so weak we seem, by our anxieties, to believe that God is not capable of taking care of us. We say that God cares, but does he? We are told God's way will work out, but will it? Anxiously we turn away from faith and trust with worry and eventually to fear. When faith and trust go, our ability to carry on goes with them. A patient who'd been in hospital for some little time was once asked by his friend who was visiting him, 'How long will you have to be in this position?' Back came the reply, 'Just one day at a time'. He'd learnt the secret.

Whenever you're oppressed by fear and doubt try to keep a close watch on your thoughts. If you dwell on depressing things you'll only breed and intensify your anxieties. Think sound, healthy, and wholesome thoughts whenever you can—those which centre on hope and faith, courage and good will. Treasure that wonderful prescription of St Paul's: 'And now, my friends, all that is true, all that is noble, all that is just and pure, all that is lovable and gracious, whatever is excellent and admirable—fill all your thoughts with these things' (Phil. 4.8). If you're prepared

33

to take that advice it will help you to trust rather than to fear, to hope rather than to despair.

The more you worry the more tense you become. It's all rather a vicious circle, isn't it? If only you can learn to relax and 'let go' you'll find that you'll become more calm, and will gradually lose the tension which fear induces. In other words 'Cast all your cares on him, for you are his charge' (1 Pet. 5.7).

Difficult as it sometimes is, try always to be thankful. Acts of thanksgiving will also help to banish many of your fears. Whatever our circumstances there is always something for which we can be thankful. 'There's always a glory in the grey', one of the poets once put it. You can thank God for the good times you've had in the midst of all the bad times you're having at present. 'O ye Light *and Darkness*, bless ye the Lord.' There is a credit side as well as a debit to life's balance sheet, and we are all very exceptional people indeed if our blessings don't outnumber our discouragements. Whenever we are despondent it is good to take a walk among our mercies. As intercession is a remedy for self-pity, so thanksgiving is a remedy for low spirits. Those words of the old hymn still ring true:

Count your blessings, name them one by one;
Count your blessings, see what God hath done;
Count your blessings, name them one by one,
And it will surprise you what the Lord hath done.

There are so many blessings to be recalled—many years of good health perhaps, the blessings of friendships, acts of kindness and sympathy, the love of one's family, the skill of doctors, the patience of nurses. We can often relearn many of the graces of gratitude and thanksgiving on a bed of pain.

Finally, may I try to help you over the fear of the unknown which is very real to us all. When you think about it there have been many experiences throughout our lives when we have been faced with fears and dreads of the unknown—when we went to a new school or when we got married, when we moved house to live in a new area or undertook new work. All these experiences were at the time rather threatening, and it was but natural for us to feel apprehensive and somewhat fearful about them. Each new day is an hitherto unvisited country which we enter, for life is pioneering; a continuous adventure into the unknown. When we now look back upon them we see that we were able to work through them and overcome them. What was so frightening proved to be life-giving and challenging once we made the change. So too with this final fear of the great unknown—our last adventure. In death we are completing the process of change and shall be moving out of the temporal into the eternal; out of the partial into the permanent.

I once read a story, very simple in its way, yet I hope meaningful in its message. It was about a doctor leaving the bedside of a patient who was very ill. As he was going the sick man stopped him and said, 'Doctor, I want to ask you a question. Am I going to get well again?' The doctor hesitated for a moment, and the sick man went on: 'Don't treat me as a child. I have a right to know. Tell me!' 'Well,' said the doctor, 'you may possibly recover this time but the next attack is pretty sure to be fatal.' The sick man caught the doctor's coat and said to him: 'Doctor, I'm afraid to die. Tell me, what lies on the other side?' Very quietly the doctor said, 'I don't know.' 'You don't know. You, a Christian man, don't know what lies beyond death?' From the other side of the door came the sound of scratching and whining. The doctor opened it, and a dog sprang into the room and leaped on him, wagging its tail and with every sign of gladness. Turning to the patient the doctor said, 'Look at this dog. He has never been in this room before. He did not know what was inside. He knew nothing except that his master was here, and as soon as I opened the door, he sprang in without fear. I know little of what is on the other side of death, but I do know one thing. I know that my Master is there,

35

and that's enough. And when the door opens I shall pass through quite fearlessly and with great gladness.' Pray that such faith and confidence may be yours.

TALK SIX
Your Family

It is only natural that you are concerned about the members of your family who are visiting you each day. When we're seriously ill our relatives often need help in dealing with the situation and coping with their own feelings. I know that you're thinking about them at this time, and perhaps wondering how they're managing at home without you. It's important that you feel part of their lives still and share in their host of emotions.

Family members often suffer if they can't express their anxieties and fears, and there's genuine and mutual relief when there's an openness about things. No longer does each member of your family have to be guarded in what he or she says. Where there's pretence this can so easily lead to tension and deceit. Openness will often become a treasured experience. You can now share together not only the sadness but also the joys that truth itself allows to break through. You can look back over good and happy memories rather than look forward to some unimagined future.

You will find those who witness suffering and pain sometimes have feelings of guilt. They feel so helpless and inadequate, and you've probably heard them say more than once: 'We wish there was something more we could do!' You'll be doing a great deal to relieve them of these feelings of frustration if you can explain to them that they are helping you most by 'just being with you', in quietness and stillness at the bedside. Frenzied activity and fussiness only serve to make matters worse. As well as outward activity and busyness, which are of course sometimes necessary, there is also an inner activity, and it is this that is expressive of hope and healing, of sympathy and love. If only you and your family can think deeply and love deeply together there'll be no need of words.

May I say a little to you about the value of silence? Unfortunately these days many people become embarrassed during periods of quiet and stillness. Noise as you know has become so much part of our make-up. Sickness can sometimes be a wonderful opportunity for silence and peace; to wait upon God. Mother Teresa of Calcutta, about whom I'm sure you've heard, once said that 'we need to find God and he cannot be found in noise and restlessness. God is a friend of silence.' You don't always feel like talking, and just being quiet together with your family helps everyone to be relaxed, for silence can often be far more creative and meaningful than words. I'm sure you don't chatter all the time when you're at home as a family, and it's not at all necessary to do so in the atmosphere of a hospital ward during visiting-times. Indeed the more of the normal home environment you can instil in the ward the better. In my visiting of hospitals I often see the wife of a patient sitting alongside her husband's bed busy knitting just as if they were together in the lounge at home; or a husband reading his paper while his wife relaxes and rests on her bed. Very few words are spoken but the depth of the relationship and intimacy are obvious. All the deeper experiences of life seem to be beyond the power of speech. The most moving moments of our lives find us all without words. True silence always seems full of holy presence.

Have you ever thought how silent our Lord was throughout his passion; how still his mother, Mary, was when standing at the foot of the cross? Such silence as that isn't a negative attitude by any means. It's rather an inner calm —a holy readiness to meet whatever comes. I'm sure you know the words of that lovely hymn which runs:

> Drop Thy still dews of quietness,
> Till all our strivings cease.
> Take from our souls the strain and stress,
> And let our ordered lives confess
> The beauty of Thy peace.

The members of your family have been telling me that they'd sensed for some little time that you'd not seemed yourself, and very naturally they kept these feelings to themselves. I'm sure you'll appreciate that their feelings of guilt and of unresolved tension sometimes make it difficult for them to communicate intimately and freely with you. They too need a listener for they often feel lonely and isolated themselves. In one sense they are patients too, with anxieties to be expressed and needs to be cared for. If everyone keeps a stiff-upper-lip attitude and adopts a false bravado it's not going to help at all. It's for this very reason that I usually like to spend some time with them when they're in hospital visiting you.

They've been made aware that because you are at present very ill you may from time to time be rather sleepy or drowsy as a result of the different medicines and drugs, so they'll perfectly understand if you want to sleep or just keep quiet and still. They appreciate too how keenly you must feel your present loss of independence, and it's only natural that you sometimes express it in terms of gratitude mingled with bouts of irritability. In constant pain there's a tendency for us to give way to anxiety and resentment. Pain causes anxiety and anxiety seems to aggravate pain. Where there is a good and free relationship between you and those who are caring for you such fears can, however, be kept to a minimum. Severe pain can also create feelings of apartness from others; relationships seem distant, and you may feel a threat of being unloved or a fear of being abandoned. Here again the presence of those whom you love and with whom you can talk, or merely be quiet, will help you to realize that after all you do belong and are being loved and supported and cared for; if it were otherwise your family and friends wouldn't be so frequent in their visits to you as they are. They love you and they're going to see you through.

Because they understand and accept your feelings and reactions in an atmosphere of mutual love and affection, you'll find that you're able to come to terms more easily with your serious illness. No doubt you're already finding that frequent visits by the members of your family and friends bring you much warmth and satisfaction. The best kind of love always involves a profound mutual understanding. What a relief it is, what a strength it is, when there's someone around who knows you through and through—someone who loves you. It puts new heart into you, doesn't it? You feel you simply couldn't let him or her down.

Because of your strong faith I kept the track
Whose sharp-set stones my strength had well-nigh spent;
I could not meet your eyes if I turned back,
So on I went.

Any experience of loving and being loved always brings an enchantment to life. To share anything—joys and sorrows, hopes and fears—gives a keener edge and a deeper meaning to all that happens; you feel more deeply, you live more richly.

There's a verse in the New Testament which says that 'every good gift and every perfect gift is from above, and cometh down from the Father of lights, with whom is no variableness neither shadow of turning' (Jas. 1.17). That affirmation is supremely true of love and friendship. All the best kind of human love is rooted in the love of God, because God *is* love. The experience of such God-given love helps us to understand more of God. It is of necessity immortal, and it is absurd to think that death can destroy it. Indeed quite possibly it will only reach its finest flowering in that other realm where all the limitations and frustrations of this life will be left behind.

I know too that many of your friends in your church are remembering you in their prayers. When we are weak and in pain we have to rely heavily upon the intercessions of others. What a great consolation it is to know that you are being supported and sustained by the thoughts and prayers of others at this time. I heard of someone once who, whenever he felt on top of the world, would say, 'I feel as if I'm being prayed for!' The awareness that 'two or three' are meeting together on your behalf will, I know, give you much strength and support. You are able to relax all the more once you know you are being upheld by your nearest and dearest, who are standing by, sharing as far as they are able your present suffering and pain.

In turn you can help your family to face up to your illness by sharing some of your own thoughts and feelings with them. This will encourage them to speak openly about their own anxieties and fears, and should they have any feelings of guilt these will be resolved by your frank talks together. They may be thinking they should have sent for the doctor earlier; they may be feeling they should have done much more to help you when you were fit and well. Indeed, did you but know it, they're probably experiencing similar feelings to those which you have yourself. Perhaps at the beginning they couldn't come to terms with the severity of your illness either. They probably thought that the diagnosis was wrong and the doctor mistaken. They too were probably shocked and angry when they heard the news.

It is from the sharing together of all these concerns that help is best derived. When secrets have to be kept between people who are normally open and frank with each other, artificial barriers are set up and conversation inevitably becomes trivial and meaningless. Do try if you can to be 'in tune' with the needs of your family and face up to the facts of the situation together. Where there are strong emotional strains these only result in considerable personal anxiety all around.

At the same time I want to make it plain that it's not every family that's able to converse openly about such things as death and dying. It can sometimes cause great embarrassment and discomfort. People who've never had to meet it before find it rather difficult to talk about. I'm sure you'll be able to judge for yourself what's best under the circumstances, for you know your family so well. If you're ever in doubt you can seek advice and counsel from the hospital chaplain or your local vicar or minister when he calls. Truth needn't be expressed in so many words. It can be made plain by the mere presence of your family and yourself together—just being prepared to be alongside each other, sharing unspoken thoughts and beliefs. You know they know, and they know you know the true situation, and so you've no need to talk about it at all if you and your family feel more at ease that way. Truth will gradually become plain in your relationships together.

There may be times when you may want to share your real feelings with someone other than your family, and this you can do with the one person to whom you can really relate, with whom you can be honest and with whom you feel most comfortable and at ease. If need be you can still keep up a pretence with others who prefer to reassure you that everything will work out all right.

When I came into the ward today I happened to notice that the nurse had been holding your hand. Have you ever thought how physical touch can bind you and members of your family together? Holding hands together in silence gives you the assurance that your family are with you and that they are ready to stay with you right up until the end. You and they are 'in touch', as it were. The clasp of an outstretched hand will assuage much of your fear and will help you to realize more and more that those around you are prepared to watch and pray with you. We shake hands to establish a common bond; those in love show their affection for each other by holding hands. There's a Nigerian proverb which says, 'Hold a true friend with both your hands.' Physical touch unites us with those about us in quite a mystical way. Their human presence with us seems to be a pledge of the divine presence.

The closer your relationships are with your family and friends the more essential it is that their visits to your bedside be frequent. They'll want to stay with you for as long as possible but it is to be hoped their visits will not be too prolonged, for little good is done by long hours of vigil at the bedside. This can be so very tiring and exhausting for all concerned. If you sometimes feel very tired when they are with you and want to go to sleep, I'm sure they aren't going to mind very much if you say so. Short, frequent visits are always preferable. On the other hand when your visitors become very tired and tense they too must be free to have a break away from the ward, for they can so easily and innocently transmit these same feelings to you.

It's during times of severe illness and distress such as you are going through at present that relationships with friends can be strengthened and perhaps many an old wound healed. After all, no family relationships are perfect. It's an opportunity for you to 'take stock' with those who have meant most to you and gather together your mutual experiences and memories, weaving them together with love and understanding. Those around you are assuring you that you won't be left alone or abandoned, and that you need never feel a 'burden' or a 'nuisance'. In such accepting and sharing you'll find your relationships being deepened and enriched.

If your family wish, they'll probably be able to be involved in a practical way in caring for you while you are here. They've only to mention this to the ward sister or staff nurse and she'll be very pleased to show them how best they can help. For example, they can wash you if necessary. They can help feed you if you find it difficult to do it yourself. With the members of the nursing staff they can help turn you in bed, arrange your pillows, pour out a drink, hand you a tissue, and make you as comfortable as possible. These little personal touches make all the difference to your comfort, and your family will have the assurance that they're helping you in a very real and practical way.

There may be a very comfortable relatives' room not far from your ward where your family are able to sleep overnight if necessary, and arrangements can probably be made for them to have their meals in the hospital restaurant. Sometimes, too, families in the area are ready to make provision for patients' friends to stay in a home atmosphere, and yet be accessible to spend time in the hospital and be near should any emergencies arise. These arrangements have probably already been explained to your family and they'll help put your mind at ease that they are being well looked after.

I want to leave you with the assurance that all that can be done for both your family and yourself is being done. All of us are with you and will be meeting your needs as far as is humanly possible. I hope such an assurance will bring you both comfort and relief.

Your Material Affairs

You may recall that in a previous talk we were reminding ourselves that to prepare for death is a Christian duty
and a Christian privilege. A sense of completion can only
be achieved when we have put our affairs in order and made
adequate provision for those we leave behind. As Christians
we should as far as possible make sure that both our
worldly affairs and our own spiritual life are always properly in order so that we are never totally unprepared for
death when it comes. Everyone should make a will, and
ideally it should have been done 'whilst we are in health',
as the Prayer Book rubric puts it.

If however you are one of the people who have delayed,
you can now go about remedying the omission. A will is
a technical, legal document, and unless it is drawn up
properly there can be room for loopholes and misinter-
pretations. These can so easily lead to family wrangles
and indeed in some instances to long and expensive court
cases in order to get things sorted out. A will has to be
signed and witnessed properly and to state in a precise
and clear-cut way what your requirements and wishes are.

A will is quite legal if drawn out simply on a piece of
paper and signed and witnessed. A printed form can be
purchased at a stationer's and details can be filled in the
relevant blank spaces and signed as the form directs. For
example where a husband leaves all his estate to his wife
and vice versa, each appointing the other as sole executor
and trustee, the form is perfectly adequate. If you do wish
to make your own will it is very important to follow
strictly the advice printed on the form, especially the sign-
ing and the witnessing necessary under the Wills Act. This
provides that the will must be signed in the presence of
two witnesses. The witnesses must also add their addresses
and occupations. It is not necessary for them to read its

contents, but you and they must sign in the presence of each other. Any persons may act as witnesses provided they understand fully what they are doing.

It is, however, always safer to have legal help which will eliminate all risk of misunderstanding and errors. It is well worth the cost of a solicitor's fee to have everything drawn out in a correct legal manner. Indeed, a solicitor will be essential should you have property or a business, derive an income from a family trust, if you are living apart from your husband or wife, or if there are any complicated financial or family situations which have to be taken into account.

You will, of course, have to make up your mind (if you have not already done so) how you want your property to be divided. It will be helpful to draw up a list of those people whom you would see as beneficiaries. There may be specific items of particular sentimental belongings you wish certain of them to have after your death, or you may wish to allocate them a sum of money each. There may be certain charities you have supported throughout the years and there is now opportunity for them to be bequeathed part of your estate. A Christian's will should also include some bequest to the Church as a thank-offering. What is left over and above after the disposal of certain items and sums of money (i.e. the residue) can either be given to some named person, divided among a number of people, or invested and perhaps the income paid to a wife or children.

Before the will is drawn up you have to decide on executors, who will see that all the transactions are carried out satisfactorily. Who are the most suitable persons to act as your executors? If your husband or wife is going to be the chief beneficiary, he or she should have some responsibility in the administration of the will. If you have grown-up children one of them might well act as co-executor. Again, a near relation or close friend might serve as a co-executor, or you might decide to have a solicitor. In certain circumstances a bank will act as executor.

As well as the concern about the disposal of your property

46

you also need to express your wish about the disposal of your body after death—i.e., burial or cremation—and to have left instructions regarding arrangements to be made about the funeral (what special hymns if any you wish to be sung, or whether flowers are to be sent). You may feel inclined to donate your body for medical research. Such requests are dealt with by H.M. Inspector of Anatomy (16/19 Greese Street, London W.1). Make sure first that your executors or next of kin know about your wish, either by having it written into your will or by leaving details among your papers. If you are married with young children and your husband or wife has already died, it is expedient to make arrangements for a suitable guardian to be appointed to look after them.

It is always wise to include a phrase in your will to the effect that any previous wills are revoked. Family and relations may sometimes wonder whether you have drawn up a will prior to the present one, and so will be saved such unnecessary concern. A second will does not automatically revoke the first.

Should you fail to make a will, what property you have will then be divided among your family. If your possessions are worth less than £15,000 and you are married, all will go to your husband or wife. If your estate is worth more, your partner will receive all personal effects, together with the first £15,000 from whatever policies, stocks and shares, bank accounts, house, etc. you possessed. What remains over is divided into two; the one half is given equally to your children, the other goes to your husband or wife in interest for life. If you have no surviving partner the estate is shared equally among your children. If you are unmarried and have not made a will your property will be divided between your parents. Should they themselves have deceased, your brothers and sisters will share it. If you are unmarried and have no relations at all, and have not made a will, your estate goes to the crown.

It is important that you explain to your dependents what insurance policies you may have, and where savings certificates, investments, and the deeds of your house are kept. It is also necessary for them to know where your will is and the place in which you keep the keys of your drawers and cabinets as well as how you wish your personal belongings, books, papers, clothing, and personal things of sentimental value to be disposed and distributed.

You may wish to donate your organs so that someone else's life may be saved. There are some organs of the body—e.g., kidneys—which can be transplanted into the body of another patient if they are removed promptly after death. Eyes can be bequeathed for corneal grafting to help cure blindess or defective sight. You can express your wishes to the ward sister and also inform your next of kin who will see that your instructions are carried out.

You will derive much satisfaction in making sure your practical affairs are now in order and that provision has been made for your family and friends. Jesus himself made provision for his mother, Mary, to be looked after, as he himself hung on the cross. St John describes it in his Gospel (19.25–7). I'll read it to you: 'Meanwhile near the cross where Jesus hung stood his mother, with her sister, Mary wife of Clopas, and Mary of Magdala. Jesus saw his mother, with the disciple whom he loved standing beside her. He said to her, "Mother, there is your son"; and to the disciple, "There is your mother"; and from that moment the disciple took her into his home.'

Your Spiritual Preparation 1

Now that you have put your material affairs in order and have made your will, let us spend some little time together discussing how best you can prepare spiritually. When you think about it there seems no event in life for which, as a rule, we prepare so scantily as for death. The story of the king and the jester which prefaces this series of talks is fairly typical of the attitude of most of us, don't you think? If there's a birthday in the family we spend time busily planning, making preparations in good time, thinking about presents, so that when the day arrives all will be in order. Well, the early Christians spoke of death as a 'birth-day'—they wore white and sang alleluias. Alleluias, for they saw it not as 'death' but as a new 'birth'—not 'farewell' but 'happy birth-day'.

What preparations can you therefore be making at this time? Well, a good life is the safe way to a good death, and a good death the sure goal of a good life. We mustn't separate the act of dying from the act of living. 'Holy living' is a necessary preparation for 'holy dying'. In one sense of course we prepare for death as soon as we are born. The New Testament teaches us that if we want to talk about death we must start by talking about life. There's a rather lovely passage in *The Prophet* by Kahlil Gibran which runs:

You would know the secret of death,
But how shall you find it unless you seek it in the heart
    of life?
The owl, whose night-bound eyes are blind unto
    the day, cannot unveil the mystery of light.
If you would indeed behold the spirit of death,
    Open your heart wide into the body of life,
For life and death are one, even as the river and the sea
    are one.

From the Christian point of view real dying always involves living and real living always involves dying. The Christian life is not so much a preparation for death as for death's destruction. The Christian does not prepare to die; he prepares not to die but to live after death.

You can prepare for death by learning to detach yourself. You can even rehearse your dying whilst living by developing daily the art of 'letting go' or 'detaching yourself', so that you will be the more ready to hand yourself over completely and confidently to God when your time comes. 'Father, into thy hands I commend my spirit.' It is often more true than we sometimes realize that 'in the midst of life we are in death'. 'By dying daily we live most fully.' In the past you may have had to 'die' in failing to achieve some long-cherished ambition: in leaving childhood behind; in seeing your children grow up and leave home to marry and live their own independent lives; in facing retirement. In all these various ways you have, all unawares perhaps, been rehearsing your dying, and when your final 'loss' or 'detachment' comes you are then all the more prepared and ready. In one sense therefore you can do much of your essential dying before your actual death occurs.

Again your preparations will prompt you to be selective. We should all be more selective and concentrated than we are. When we read the Gospels we are struck by our Lord's tremendous concentration and singleness of purpose. It was surely because the thought of his death was ever before him that when it came it didn't find him unprepared. So with ourselves—you and I have to make the most of the opportunities for promoting and strengthening our own spiritual lives, our service for others, and for the setting forward of the greater glory of God. We have to concentrate on the things that really matter in life; we have to learn how to 'eliminate the inessentials', so that when our call comes we may be able to say: 'My work is finished—though I have done little, that little has been my best.'

May I remind you of three most essential parts of your immediate preparation for death. Death is really a sacramental experience and preparation for it should be the same as for all the other sacraments, so penitence, charity, and faith are very important conditions to be achieved. Broadly speaking you can say that penitence has to do with your feelings, charity with your will, and faith with your mind, so together they express your wholeness as a person. They are not, of course, three separate entities; they inter-relate and interact and none can be there without the others.

I should like to spend a little time talking to you about each of them in turn. Let's think about faith first of all. Faith means putting your whole trust and confidence in God. Where there is faith we can do all things through him who strengthens us, for faith is our utter reliance upon God, accepting whatever he thinks best for us. It may be life, it may be death—yet whichever it is we shall be at peace within ourselves. Whatever happens to you it means you still believe in him, still trust him, still are certain of his love for you. In the midst of the most adverse circumstances faith can still say, 'My Lord and my God'. Nothing is beyond God's control. God is still in command. If we really believe that, we can take our troubles to him and leave the issue in his hands. We are not to tell God our worries, and then go on worrying as if we had never gone to him at all, or as if he had refused to help us. That is not faith but faithlessness. 'Have no anxiety about anything', says St Paul, 'but in everything by prayer and supplication let your requests be made known to God' (Phil. 4.6); and then this result will follow: 'The peace of God which passes all understanding, will keep your hearts and minds in Christ Jesus' (Phil. 4.7).

Faith is not trying to explain your situation or explain it away; it is being ready to carry it with perfect confidence into the presence of God. It means you can always count on his presence and his help, whatever may be your need, or whatever may be the emergency. Faith is that certainty that in good times or bad, in sorrow or in joy, he is with you and his presence always transforms the situation. Those words of Psalm 139 should do much to help you. I shall read them to you:

> If I climb into heaven, thou art there: if I go down to hell, thou art there also.

> If I take the wings of the morning: and remain in the uttermost parts of the sea; even there also shall thy hand lead me: and thy right hand shall hold me.

If ever you are worried by what you regard to be a lack of faith on your part, never be afraid to lean on the faith of those around you—those who are nursing you, seeing to your daily needs, your family and friends—as well as the faith of the Church which is continually surrounding and strengthening you with love and prayer. Here's a short act of faith which you may like to repeat from time to time:

> I believe in God the Father who has made me
> and all the world.
> I believe in God the Son who has redeemed me
> and all mankind.
> I believe in God the Holy Spirit who sanctifies me
> and all the elect people of God.

> Lord, I believe.
> Help thou my unbelief.

Faith fills us with hope. When the body becomes weak it sometimes makes our spirits weak as well. We find it difficult to keep up our faith and effort in prayer seems impossible. In times like these Christ comes to us with his message of hope—'My strength is made perfect in weakness.' The more we realize our own weakness the more Christ is prepared to reveal his strength. You will discover that when you find hope difficult, God comes to you; there is no need for you to go to God. It is sometimes better not to try to make a great effort but merely to wait quietly upon God. It is the prayer of us all that 'The God of hope [may] fill you with all joy and peace by your faith in him, until, by the power of the Holy Spirit, you overflow with hope' (Rom. 15.13). Such hope will enable you to place yourself wholeheartedly in his care, submit yourself to his love, and resign yourself to his wisdom.

Oh my God, I hope in you for grace and for glory, because of your promises, your mercy and your power.

Lord, in thee have I trusted.
Let me never be confounded.

As part of your preparation for death there will be the need for unselfishness, for generous thought for others, and an outgoing spirit towards both God and people. There will be consideration for all those who are ministering to your needs at this time, and by intercession for those who will be left behind; there will be deep gratitude and thanksgiving towards God for the gift of your life here and the promise of the life to come. You will thank him for looking after you throughout the past and for the promise and assurance of his care for the future.

Shall I read you some parts of St Paul's great chapter on 'Charity' from 1 Corinthians 13?

Though I speak with the tongues of men and of angels, and have not charity ... I am nothing ... Charity suffereth long, and is kind; charity envieth not; charity vaunteth not itself, is not puffed up, Doth not behave itself unseemly, seeketh not her own, is not easily provoked, thinketh no evil; Rejoiceth not in iniquity but rejoiceth in the truth; Beareth all things, believeth all things, hopeth all things, endureth all things. Charity never faileth.

Charity is the love that doesn't have to be earned by any merit or reward—it is spontaneous. It is a love that gives in the spirit of complete unselfishness. There is

53

nothing sloppy or sentimental about it, and it's a shame that with the passing of the years the word 'charity' has lost a great deal of its loveliness in our everyday speech.

> And now abideth faith, hope, charity, these three; but the greatest of these is charity.
>
> 1 Cor. 13.13

While:

> Faith will vanish into sight;
> Hope be emptied in delight,
> Love in heaven will shine more bright;
> Therefore give us love.
>
> *Hymns Ancient and Modern Revised*, 233

We shall now make an act of love together:

> O my God, I desire to love you because you only are holy and worthy of love: Help me to love you with all my heart, and my neighbour as myself.

> Jesus, my Lord, I you adore,
> O make me love you more and more.

TALK NINE
Your Spiritual Preparation 2

When we are lying on our backs in bed there's only one place to look and that's up. It is in such moments that we think and ponder and reflect on our past lives. 'Have I thought much about God?' 'How much do I really love him?' 'Have I said my prayers as regularly as I should have?' 'Have I forgiven everyone I would wish?' 'Is there anything for which I myself would like to be forgiven?' 'Are there sins which are particularly worrying me at this time?' 'What sort of a Christian have I really been?'

There are very few of us indeed who are entirely satisfied with our past and present lives. There was once a Christmas party being given in a church hall for children who were physically handicapped. A little girl was seen crying outside the door, who when asked what the trouble was replied: 'I can't get in because there's nothing the matter with me!' To think that we have nothing the matter with us bars our entrance to the presence of Christ. 'If we say that we have no sin,' said the disciple, 'we deceive ourselves, and the truth is not in us. If we confess our sins he is faithful and just to forgive us our sins, and to cleanse us from all unrighteousness' (1 John 1.8–9). Ask the Holy Spirit to give you the light of truth to examine your life, for without his light you will most certainly deceive yourself. Each of us will use different schemes for this work of self-examination. You can use the one which you find most helpful, knowing that no sins are too big and none too little for his forgiveness. We sometimes excuse ourselves by saying things like, 'I'm no worse than anyone else!' 'People seem to like me, so I can't be so bad after all'. What we have to realize of course is that God will judge us not by the standard of public opinion but by the standard of his only son, Jesus Christ. When we picture him on his cross we soon realize there is no room left in us for complacency.

> He died that we might be forgiven,
> He died to make us good.

He who hangs there willingly endured that awful death that we might be forgiven. From the cross he comes to us: 'This is what I have done for your sake. Will you not forgive one another for my sake.' Remember 'thou shalt call his name Jesus, for he shall save his people from their sins' (Matt. 1.21). We have to stand afar off as it were with the publican and echo his prayer: 'God be merciful to me a sinner' (Luke 18.13).

Penitence is really saying to God: 'I'm sorry'. It's putting yourself right with God. When we sin we are out of touch with him and it is penitence which puts us back in touch with him again. Feeling sorry, however, is no substitute for being sorry, and it's so easy to delude ourselves about this. To be genuinely sorry for our sins requires three ingredients. First you must face the particular sins for which you are responsible and know what they are. Second, you must own up to them and accept responsibility; and finally you must ask God to forgive you in order that you can begin again to live a holy life and die a happy death.

Please don't misunderstand me. I don't want you to force yourself to think and brood over all the bad and mean and silly things you might have done. God does not want you to wallow in your wrongdoings, but because he is holy as well as loving, your confession of your sins and seeking his forgiveness should have a natural place in your life. Concentrate your thoughts on Christ and not on yourself. It is right for you to be concerned with your sins, but you mustn't become obsessed by them. It will help if you look outwards towards Christ and inwards towards yourself. If you only look at him long enough and seriously enough he will by his very nature reveal to you the sins he wants you to confess. There is therefore no need to be burrowing deeply into your soul, stirring muddy waters, and becoming more and more disturbed by your search for your sins. Rather lift up your heart and look at him. Your examination of conscience will then become less of a check-list and more of a prayer: less a matter of asking yourself: 'What have I done wrong?' than of asking God: 'How do I stand before you, Lord?' He doesn't expect from you the impossible, and you are not obliged to do more than try to make mention of your chief sins in thought, word, and deed. He will then draw you to himself and in his light sufficient insight will be given you to see into the darkness of your heart.

Always remember that God is full of love for you and far more ready to forgive you than you are to repent. Unless the prodigal son had been absolutely certain of his father's love he would have never resolved to say: 'I will arise and go to my father, and will say unto him, Father, I have sinned' (Matt. 15.18). Do bear in mind the tender fatherly love of God and believe that you haven't to persuade him to be merciful and forgiving. 'When he was yet a great way off, his father saw him, and had compassion, and ran, and fell on his neck, and kissed him' (Matt. 15.20). So too is he longing to receive you and give you the kiss of forgiveness.

When you use the Lord's Prayer you say: 'Forgive us our trespasses as we forgive them that trespass against us.' God keeps before us the reminder that we can only hope for forgiveness if we ourselves are prepared to be forgiving. Before we can repeat that petition for ourselves we must do our very best to let the spirit of charity and forgiveness take possession of our hearts. You have heard, as I have heard, people sometimes say: 'I will forgive, but I can never forget' or 'I'm prepared to forgive him but we can never be the same to each other again!' This of course is forgiveness in mere words: it is really not forgiveness at all. I wonder where we'd be all be if God's forgiveness of us went no further than that? No, our forgiveness must be like his—righteous and real.

I wonder if there is anyone whom you have wronged

in the past, or perhaps members of the family circle with whom you have broken off relationships because of some 'tiff' or quarrel? Is there any person (or persons) from whom you have become estranged ('He treated me so badly and said such untruths about me, I haven't wanted to have anything more to do with him')? Perhaps the action was un-called for; perhaps he did treat you badly; perhaps it was all his fault and he was in the wrong; but then so are we all sometimes. After all the forgiveness we have received who are we to withhold it from others? We have to remember our own failures, our own frequent lapses into sin, our ingratitude, our readiness to judge others harshly, and for-give as we hope to be forgiven.

If you have been a penitent in the past you will obviously want to make a final confession and to wait patiently for death to come. If you wish to make a formal confession send for the hospital chaplain and he will be pleased to make the necessary arrangements. Should you wish to see your own spiritual director the chaplain will contact him for you. You will be able, in his presence, to tell God what your sins are, as far as you can recall them, and ex-press your sorrow for them. You are then assured of God's pardon by the words of absolution of the priest. 'Our Lord Jesus Christ, who has left power to his Church to absolve all sinners who truly repent and believe in him, of his great mercy forgive you all your offences: and by his authority committed unto me, I absolve you from all your sins, in the name of the Father, and of the Son and of the Holy Spirit, Amen.' If such a formal confession is at all a strain, don't worry, for your priest will perfectly understand. When we are very ill it is hard to concentrate, often difficult to speak for long. If it should be necessary the priest will make the act of contrition himself and then grant you absolution. If you are feeling very weak, the priest will say with you a short exhortation or ejaculatory prayer—'Jesus mercy' or 'O Lamb of God that taketh away the sins of the world'. You can confidently leave everything in God's hands, for he understands and forgives.

You may not wish to make your confession to a priest, and feel you can ease your conscience by making a general and informal confession of sin. Again don't worry if it seems halting or hesitant. It is your sincerity, not your accuracy, that counts. A sincere good will is always met by free forgiveness. God knows only too well about your difficulties. He knows that the longing for forgiveness is there even when you are unable to express it. Never be discouraged if you find it impossible to put your repentance into words. Recall, if you can, some familiar phrase—e.g., 'Son of David, Jesus, have pity on me' (Mark 10.47); 'Make me a clean heart, O God: and renew a right spirit within me' (Ps. 51.10); 'Jesus, forgive me'—and try to breathe into them the intensity of your individual sorrow for sin and your longing for forgiveness, with a full trust in God's mercy. Whatever way you express and acknowledge your unworthiness you will hear him say to you: 'Today shalt thou be with me.' He will meet you with open arms, take you into his keeping, and you will be at peace. We can make an act of contrition together:

O my God, I resolve to forsake all those sins by which I have grieved you: help me by your grace to avoid occasions of sin and to sin no more: through Jesus Christ our Lord.

Your Spiritual Preparation 3

You've been telling me about some of your favourite hymns. They seem to come back to our minds at times like these, don't they? The verses we used to sing without thinking too much about the words perhaps now seem to have a deeper significance and a greater appeal. I'm sure they are going to help you. If you can't read them for yourself, the chaplain, members of your family, or one of the nurses will be ready to spend a little time reminding you of some of your favourites. There's a lovely medieval hymn in the Old Sarum Primer which makes a rather wonderful prayer, particularly the last couplet.

> God be in my head
> And in my understanding.
> God be in my eyes
> And in my looking.
> God be in my mouth
> And in my speaking.
> God be in my heart
> And in my thinking.
> God be at mine end
> And at my departing.

'Abide with Me' is a favourite with most people and is all about preparation for death. When you think of the cross or are going through a particularly 'bad patch', what consolation you can derive from that wonderful final verse:

Hold thou thy cross before my closing eyes;
Shine through the gloom, and point me to the skies:
Heaven's morning breaks, and earth's vain shadows flee;
In life, in death, O Lord, abide with me.

Hymns Ancient and Modern Revised (From now on abbreviated AMR), 27

The Cross has an everlasting appeal, for in that sign we can offer up ourselves, our pain and suffering and that of others, to Christ, not as a magic symbol but as an assurance and pledge of his presence with us. In that Christ himself was tested and tried he can help others like yourself who are going through it now.

> Nothing in my hand I bring,
> Simply to thy cross I cling.

Whenever your mind is clouded or you feel too weary to pray, the sign of the cross can be the quickest of all prayers. It is the body's prayer as it were. The sign of the cross will recall for you your baptismal promise: not to 'be ashamed to confess the faith of Christ crucified, and manfully to fight under his banner against sin, the world and the devil; and to continue Christ's faithful soldier and servant unto your life's end'. Such bodily action will influence your thoughts and mind. Keeping the cross in the centre of your life, you will be the more ready to commend yourself into the hands of your heavenly Father.

The cross brings a message to you as no other thing or being can. For it says to you: God does understand you to the full, for Christ understands you. Christ feels not only for you but with you. Christ has suffered not only for you but with you. You have to go through nothing which Christ has not gone through. He endured fear, shame, agony, and death for you that he might be touched with the feeling of your infirmity and help you to endure, and bring you safe through all to victory and to peace.

O Saviour of the World, who by your cross and passion has redeemed us, save us and help us, we humbly beseech you.

Think of the cross as regularly as you can, for it is a sermon carved in wood. It will speak to you of the wonderful love of God. It's not always easy to believe in the love of God at a time like this—it's so hard sometimes that it seems all but impossible. There are very few of us indeed who have not cried out in moments of acute bodily pain or mental stress—'Can God really love me, when he lets me suffer so much?' But listen to those words of Christ—'God so loved the world that he gave his only-begotten son.' Or those words of St Paul—'God commendeth his own love toward us, in that while we were yet sinners Christ died for us.' The death of Christ upon the cross is the everlasting proof of the love of God. God in giving us Christ gave us his all. In the face of so wonderful a proof, can we any longer doubt, in spite of all our difficulties and troubles, that God does really love us?

The greatest thing in the life of Christ, that by which he achieved most for the world, is not his teaching or his example, but his death. 'I, if I be lifted up, will draw all men unto me. This he said, signifying what death he should die.' So often the cry of the world is for an easy religion without any pain or self-denial, but the voice of Jesus calls us to a life of self-conquest and self-discipline, bidding us take up our cross and follow him. Look at the cross, then, with a grateful and penitent affection, and use the sign of the cross as often as you can. Make it not as a mere act of formal ceremonialism but with reverence and care, as an outward and visible sign of an inward devotion to Christ crucified. 'May I so meditate upon your suffering that I may learn to suffer with you.'

> When I survey the wondrous cross,
> On which the Prince of Glory died,
> My richest gain I count but loss,
> And pour contempt on all my pride.
> AMR, 108

Another helpful practice brought home to us through our favourite hymns is the invocation of the holy name. You will find that merely repeating 'Jesus, Jesus' will bring you much blessing and comfort. With perseverance you will find that the name of Jesus will come quite spontaneously to your lips and will remain in your mind, especially during times of stress or spasms of pain.

> How sweet the name of Jesus sounds
>   In a believer's ear:
> It soothes his sorrows, heals his wounds,
>   And drives away his fear.

> Till then I would thy love proclaim
>   With every fleeting breath;
> And may the music of thy name
>   Refresh my soul in death.
>
> AMR, 192

To Jesus' name you can link the names of all your loved ones—those living, those departed—so meeting in his name with all the whole company of the saints on earth and in heaven.

> Therefore we in love adoring
>   This most blessed name revere,
> Holy Jesu, thee imploring
>   So to write it in us here,
> That hereafter heavenward soaring
>   We may sing with angels there.
>
> AMR, 190

Our Lord in his suffering had great confidence in prayer. 'Being in agony he prayed.' Prayer will play an important part in your preparation. I mentioned prayer to you in an earlier talk and I said then that you haven't to feel 'good' or 'holy' or 'pious' but you have to be honest when you pray. I'd like to say more about this now, for many people get worried about their feelings when they pray. I want to make it clear that feelings are largely temperamental. They depend on all sorts of things—on whether you are tired, in pain, or worried and tense. We are to trust not our feelings about God but God himself. Whatever your feelings are, the fact is that God is where you are. Feelings are not to be trusted! God remains and you remain —so just trust him. There will be times—perhaps they'll be frequent—when you'll feel God is far away, far removed and remote from your troubles. You may get bitter and resentful, for we are all subject to moods and changes of temperament. You may feel there can be no God. I want to assure you that whether you feel he is with you or not has no bearing whatsoever on his actually being with you all the time. Your feelings are usually most unreliable guides to your relationship with God. They change from day to day, hour to hour. Whatever you may feel—remember God is always with you and in you.

Try to adopt an attitude of perfect dependence in prayer, surrendering yourself utterly to God no matter what the outcome will be. Just place yourself at God's disposal so that he can do with you and in you what he wills. Pray that whatever you may have to suffer now you will have the power and discernment to do the will of God. When you read about our Lord's own prayers in the face of death in the garden of Gethsemane you will notice that there were three stages. First he made an act of faith in God his Father: 'Father, all things are possible to thee.' Next he asked for something for himself: 'Remove this cup from me.' Finally he offered himself up completely to the will of God: 'Yet not what I will, but what thou wilt.' This surrender he endorsed with his last breath on the cross: 'Father, into thy hands I commit my spirit.' If you wish you can use these same prayers as they stand in union with your Lord, or you can use words which come most naturally to you but including the same elements of faith, petition and surrender. Your prayer will then not be in the form of 'Please God, do for me what I want', but rather 'Please God, do with me what you want'. Such a form of prayer will always be answered in proportion to its sincerity.

In the garden of Gethsemane we also read of our Lord praying the same prayer over and over again. We must not lose patience nor expect quick and easy results. 'He spoke to them ... that they should keep on praying and never lose heart' (Luke 18.1). Our Lord repeated 'Thy will be done' through the whole of the night. Your only prayer can be the Lord's Prayer, no matter how long it takes you to say it. The prayer in Gethsemane was but the repetition between long silences of one single petition. Nightly as you prepare to sleep you can say, 'Into thy hands I commend my spirit'; at your last sleep you will be ready to give up your spirit to God, and death itself becomes an offering to God.

You will find these short ejaculatory or 'arrowhead' prayers will help you rest your weakness on God's strength. 'God is here.' 'God is love.' 'I come from God, I belong to God, I go to God.' 'Jesus is with me.' 'Jesus is in me.' They will help you to become more and more sensitive to God's presence. You will be letting God, who is already within you, take hold of you and keep you in his peace. 'O my God, I believe in you. O my God, I love you. O my God, I am sorry for my sins. O my God, I offer you my sufferings. Jesus, Saviour, I give you my heart.'

Periods of silence and stillness will give you opportunity to wait upon God. 'They that wait upon the Lord shall renew their strength.' When you listen, God speaks. In silence you can 'wait patiently for him', and you will be meeting him within the secret stillness of your heart. 'Speak Lord, for thy servant heareth.' 'Thou wilt keep him in perfect peace whose mind is stayed on thee.' 'In quietness and confidence shall be your strength.' There will be many distractions in a hospital ward, but do remember that if your thoughts wander from him, his thoughts do not wander from you.

May I leave another thought with you: when you pray you are never praying alone. However personal your prayers are they are always forming part of a much bigger whole—the Church, the Body of Christ, and the Passion of Christ. The loneliness of praying on your own will be overcome as soon as you realize you are one in a great company which no man can number. 'Let *us* pray.' In your prayers you are surrounded by angels and archangels and the whole company of heaven. What a wonderful thought that is.

TALK ELEVEN
Bible Readings

Bible-reading will also form part of our preparation for death. The Scriptures teach us not only the best way of living but also the most comfortable way of dying.

> Word of mercy, giving
> Succour to the living;
> Word of life, supplying
> Comfort to the dying.
>
> AMR, 250

May I offer you three practical suggestions about your Bible-reading? Be selective in the passages you read or have read to you. Be as regular as your sickness will allow, and try to live out the passage at hand. What do these verses say to me in my present predicament? How can I best apply them to the circumstances I find myself in?

> O may these heavenly pages be
>   My ever dear delight,
> And still new beauties may I see
>   And still increasing light.
>
> AMR, 251

Oftentimes all that will be necessary will be to hold a favourite verse or phrase in your mind. The chaplain or members of your family will most willingly read to you from the Gospel stories, or prayers or psalms. Let the reading be full of hope, of praise, of thanksgiving. 'Did not our hearts burn within us as he spoke to us on the way ... and explained the Scriptures to us'. I shall leave with you the references of some selected passages which I'm sure you will find useful, particularly at times when you are tired, in pain, afraid, discouraged, or under stress (see pp. 129–37).

One method of Bible-reading is to read one of the healing

miracles in the Gospels and make from it a kind of litany for those around you. 'O Jesus, who *looked* with compassion upon the sick man, look with compassion too upon this hospital and its wards and departments, on all patients here who are facing operations today, on those who are in special need of our prayers at this time. O Jesus, who *touched* the sick man, let those in pain and weariness feel your healing touch. Touch with your healing hands those who minister to them and grant them skill, patience, and understanding. May they go about their work with gentleness and compassion. O Jesus, who *spoke* to the sick man, speak to all those who are on my ward, especially those who are finding it difficult to maintain their faith and to realize your presence.' There are many other incidents in the gospel which you can apply to your scheme of intercession.

The psalter was our Lord's own treasury of devotion. Twice he uttered words from the psalms as he hung on the cross. Let's think, shall we, of some of the words which he spoke. They have become known as the 'Seven Words' from the cross.

1. 'Father, forgive them for they know not what they do' (Luke 23.34). We, too, should be found asking pardon for our sins, and freely forgiving any who have offended us. 'Father' was a name which our Lord was never tired of repeating. In all his pain and suffering his Father was very near—and very real—to him. In the dark hour of the cross his thoughts and prayers were more for others than for himself. Do I forgive as I hope to be forgiven? Do I pray for those whom I dislike, or for those I find it difficult to get on with?

2. 'Verily I say unto you, Today shalt thou be with me in paradise' (Luke 23.43). Looking forward eagerly to the blessed hope of fuller fellowship with Christ. Every syllable of this word is full of power. 'Verily'—the symbol of certainty: 'today'—the symbol of compassion: 'Thou shalt be with me'—the symbol of generosity. My hope in Christ begins on the cross today but it does not end there. Paradise can fulfil it; death can open my eyes to it.

3. 'He saith unto his mother, Woman, behold thy son! Then saith he to the disciple, Behold thy mother' (John 19.26–7). Making such provision as we can for those we leave behind. This word teaches us the blessing of friendship. How happy and fruitful our own friendships may be if we share them with our Lord. We learn the value of a good home and give thanks to all who have helped to make it so. Christ tells us that 'in my Father's house are many mansions: if it were not so, I would have told you. I go to prepare a place for you. And if I go and prepare a place for you, I will come again, and receive you unto myself; that where I am, there ye may be also' (John 14.2–3).

4. 'My God, my God, why hast thou forsaken me?' (Mark 15.34). Trusting through despondency and spiritual depression, in the certainty that God has not forsaken us. This word of desolation can be for us the word of consolation. It assures you of Christ's sympathy—he can sympathize with you from experience in your times of despondency and spiritual depression. Times come to most of us when we seem to lose conviction; when we are faced with the horrible suspicion that our faith has grown cold; when the sacraments seem mere outward forms, and prayer void of inward grace. In moments such as these what courage and comfort we may find when we turn our eyes to the cross, clinging to him in our hours of darkness and crying out as he did—'My God, My God'—in spite of everything that makes us feel forsaken. Always remember that ours is a suffering God who knows what it is to be unable to see the sunshine of God's presence for the clouds.

5. 'I thirst' (John 19.28). The word of desire, patiently accepting the ministry of others. Eager for sacramental communion with our Lord, and for the refreshment of his presence. He thirsts to bless you, to save you, to supply your every need. He thirsts too for your love, your trust, and your obedience. It is in the power of every one of us to minister to him. Each of us can offer him the cup of our own heart, brimming over with penitence, gratitude, and faith. 'Those who hunger and thirst after righteousness shall be filled' (Matt. 5.6).

6. 'It is finished' (John 19.30). Laying our marred life with all its shortcomings on the one and perfect finished work of Jesus. This is the word of triumph. 'I have glorified thee on the earth: I have finished the work which thou gavest me to do' (John 17.4). Christ conquers death in three ways. He proves it is not the end of existence, but only an incident in continuing life, 'a bend on the road which leads the traveller home'. He takes away the loneliness of death, and he removes its sting which is sin. The first of these he achieved for us by his resurrection, the other two by his finished work on the cross. He too, like you, has grappled with loneliness, and he promises to be your companion in that last hour. 'Lo, I am with you alway, even unto the end of the world' (Matt. 28.20). If only you can hold his cross before your eyes, and have his presence in your heart, then you need never fear death. You may look forward calmly to that tremendous experience knowing that he, the eternal God, is your refuge, and underneath you are his everlasting arms.

7. 'Father, into thy hands I commend my spirit' (Luke 23.46). Entrusting ourselves for all eternity to the love and faithfulness of our heavenly Father. This is the word of peace. It is the attitude of willing surrender. It was not death which approached Christ, but Christ who approached death. We see here the note of complete certainty of the future life. 'I am the resurrection, and the life' (John 11.25). 'Death is swallowed up in victory' (1 Cor.

15.54). If such be your spirit you need not fear to die, for instead of thinking of death as ending you will think of life as beginning and that more abundantly. Instead of thinking of losing you will think of gaining; instead of parting you will be meeting. May each one of us, when the time comes, be prepared to commit ourselves to the love of God, humbly echoing Christ's words of perfect trust and confidence—'Father, into thy hands I commend my spirit.'

Or you may like to take a particular psalm and think about it. Remembering that the favourite and best known and loved of all the psalms is the twenty-third psalm about the Good Shepherd, let's read it together verse by verse and think about its meaning. I'm going to use the familiar version—we're all more used to that, and it brings out the beauty and simplicity of the psalm in a very special way. It has a most precious and significant message in times of sickness for it's full of the feeling of being loved and cared for by God; it speaks of peace and certainty.

1. 'The Lord is my Shepherd; therefore can I lack nothing.' Let's think about that word 'shepherd'. The first thought is that the sheep belong to him. Some words of another psalm bring this home to us:

> Know ye that the Lord he is God: it is he that hath made us, and not we ourselves; we are his people, and the sheep of his pasture.
>
> Ps. 100.3

The sheep belong to the shepherd, and the shepherd wants his sheep. God made us: we belong to him; and he wants us. What a very comforting thought that is.

> The King of Love my Shepherd is,
>   Whose goodness faileth never;
> I nothing lack if I am his
>   And he is mine for ever.
>
> AMR, 197

70

He has made me because he wants me, and he it is who shepherds me and takes care of me. Therefore we ought to trust him fully. Whenever you can, make an act of faith in his all-wise and all-sheltering love, and thank him for all the perils, known and unknown, from which he has saved you.

He shall feed his flock like a shepherd: he shall gather the lambs with his arm, and carry them in his bosom.

Isa. 40.11

Because the Lord is your shepherd 'therefore you will lack nothing', for he is always watching over you and always near at hand when you want him.

2. 'He shall feed me in a green pasture: and lead me forth beside the waters of comfort.' The green pastures are a symbol of God's bountiful provision for all your needs. They assure you that God cares for you and wills to supply you with what you want at this time.

The Scottish metrical version of the psalm runs:

> The Lord my pasture shall prepare,
> And feed me with a shepherd's care;
> His presence shall my wants supply,
> And guard me with a watchful eye;
> My noonday walks he shall attend,
> And all my midnight hours defend.

You will be supplied with all you need in your sickness if only you will trust him, and wait upon him. Take special note of the fact, too, that it is at noontide, when the heat is greatest and the toil most burdensome, that you are to find his refreshment. It is in the heat of the day when perhaps your pain is at its peak that he, the Good Shepherd, will lead you to a more shaded and sheltered spot. He will lead you to streams at the side of which you'll be able to rest from time to time. He says to you: 'Whosoever drinketh of the water that I shall give him shall never thirst; but the water that I shall give

71

him shall be in him a well of water springing up into everlasting life' (John 4.14). 'If any man thirst, let him come unto me, and drink' (John 7.37). 'I am come that they may have life, and may have it abundantly' (John 10.10). Follow him then—the Shepherd—until he brings you to 'the green pasture' and 'the still waters', for the heart of the Shepherd is most simple, patient, loving, and understanding.

3. 'He shall convert my soul: and bring me forth in the paths of righteousness for his name's sake.' The verb 'convert' means to 'revive' or 'refresh'. The Good Shepherd is leading you and cries to you: 'Come unto me, all ye that labour and are heavy laden, and I will give you rest' (Matt. 11.28). If you are prepared to follow him along the way of humble trust and obedience he becomes your companion and bears the yoke with you; and you will soon find rest and refreshment. 'Take my yoke upon you', he says, 'and learn of me; for I am meek and lowly in heart: and ye shall find rest unto your souls' (Matt. 11.29). Take him at his word and trust him, and do what he tells you. As the Good Shepherd he knows where to lead you, and he isn't going to take you anywhere where there is no pasture to be found. There will always be sufficient pasture for the day, and he will bring you safely to 'the waters of comfort' before nightfall. Acknowledge his wisdom and praise him for his love.

4. 'Yea, though I walk through the valley of the shadow of death, I will fear no evil: for thou art with me; thy rod and thy staff they comfort me.' Remind yourself it is a valley, not a cul-de-sac. Just as surely there was a way in, so surely there will be a way out. As you pass through you realize the strength in and comfort of the presence of the Shepherd, for he alone knows the way.

The words are full of meaning and of power to comfort and inspire:

The people that walked in darkness have seen a great light: they that dwell in the land of the shadow of death, upon them hath the light shined.

Isa. 9.2

The words are full of confidence:

The Lord is my light and my salvation; whom shall I fear? the Lord is the strength of my life; of whom shall I be afraid?

Ps. 27.1

Because he is with you you have no reason to fear. 'For ... thou ... art ... with ... me.' He is an arm on which you can lean when the valley seems dark and depressing. With his rod and staff he will protect you from harm and 'deliver you from evil'. His shepherd's crook will often help you to turn back to him in moments of doubt or disappointment. It will help you stop and think, to ponder and to pray.

> In death's dark vale I fear no ill
> With thee, dear Lord, beside me.
> Thy rod and staff my comfort still;
> Thy cross before to guide me.

5. 'Thou shalt prepare a table before me against them that trouble me: Thou hast anointed my head with oil, and my cup shall be full.' Are you going to trust God to see you through? There are many things that 'trouble' us—our own doubts and fears. It often requires real courage and faith to be able to say, 'I will trust God to see me through.' One of the other psalms speaks of 'the oil of gladness'.

God, thy God, hath anointed thee with the oil of gladness above thy fellows.

Ps. 45.8

Gladness is a distinctive mark of God's anointing.

They shall obtain joy and gladness, and sorrow and sighing shall flee away.

Isa. 35.10

We are meant to be glad: he wants us to be glad. When we are glad much of our depression and fear will 'flee away'. We shall find the cup of God's mercy will run over to support and strengthen us, and we shall want to say with another psalmist:

What reward shall I give unto the Lord: for all the benefits that he hath done unto me? I will receive the cup of salvation: and call upon the Name of the Lord.

Ps. 116.11–12

6. 'But thy loving-kindness and mercy shall follow me all the days of my life: and I will dwell in the house of the Lord for ever.' How immeasurably greater is the shepherd's love and care than the sheep can ever imagine! May you have sufficient understanding of God's love to rest in his 'goodness and mercy', and be at peace, even as the sheep know that they are being looked after and therefore feel that they are safe.

He shall feed his flock like a shepherd: he shall gather the lambs with his arm, and carry them in his bosom . . .

Isa. 40.11

To 'dwell in the house of the Lord' means abiding in God and holding continual communion with him.

The eternal God is thy refuge,
And underneath are the everlasting arms.

Deut. 33.27

In his 'many mansions' there will be room for all, where he will receive us unto himself, so that where he is, there we may be also.

One thing have I desired of the Lord, which I will require; even that I may dwell in the house of the Lord

74

all the days of my life, to behold the fair beauty of the Lord, and to visit his temple.

Ps. 27.4

We pray that the vision of God will one day be ours.

'For ever'—for all eternity. How grateful we should be to him for the hope of eternal life.

Jesus saith unto her, Thy brother shall rise again. Martha saith unto him, I know that he shall rise again in the resurrection at the last day. Jesus said unto her, I am the resurrection, and the life: he that believeth in me, though he were dead, yet shall he live: And whosoever liveth and believeth in me shall never die. Believest thou this? She saith unto him, Yea, Lord: I believe that thou art the Christ, the Son of God.

John 11.23–7

The Sacraments 1

In this present talk I want to mention the sacraments. They are the means whereby an inward and spiritual grace comes to us through an outward and visible sign. In the sacraments Christ himself is working—the hands of the visible priest are seen but it is the invisible priest who really does the work. There is nothing magical about them, and they won't benefit us unless we correspond as actively as we can with the grace they offer—just as food won't nourish us unless we're prepared to digest it. The other point I would like to make plain is that they are not an end in themselves, but only a means to an end, that is the development and strengthening of our spiritual lives through union with our Lord. We are given spiritual power in the sacraments that we may use it.

Now the highest means whereby we can receive his divine life into ourselves is in the sacrament of the body and blood of Christ—Holy Communion. In sickness you will find that communion with the risen Lord will bring you deep faith and tranquillity. His presence will uphold and strengthen you now and in all that may lie ahead. The more troubled and anxious you are, the more you will need to draw near to Christ in this central act of worship and give yourself, just as you are, into his hands—those wounded hands which will uplift and support you. With Christ dwelling in you and manifesting his presence to you, you will find him your 'Hope and strength, a very present help in trouble'. Receiving the sacrament, you will be able to say: 'The Lord of hosts is with us; the God of Jacob is our refuge; and if God be for us, who then can be against us?'

I wonder if you have received Holy Communion during the time you've been ill. If you are normally a regular communicant at your church at home you will want, I hope, to receive it in hospital. The Church makes special provision for those who are sick and away from their parish church, for there is 'The Communion of the Sick', which can be brought to your bedside. If you have not already asked for your Holy Communion please don't hesitate to let the hospital chaplain know and he will explain to you what form the service takes and make the necessary practical arrangements on the ward. As you are at present very ill you will need more than ever 'the strengthening and refreshing of your soul by the body and blood of Christ'. I feel certain that you will find much spiritual joy as a result of receiving the sacrament. Don't be too disappointed if you don't always feel or experience it at the time, for eucharistic joy is essentially a spiritual joy—a no mere passing convulsion of pleasure, but true joy, living joy, for 'in the presence of God there is the fulness of joy, and at his right hand there are pleasures for evermore'. The Eucharist will, I know, be to you an increasing source of grace, satisfaction, and delight, for Christ will take you in his holy hands and bless you.

Unfortunately many patients in hospital seem rather shy of asking for the sacrament to be brought to them. It seems to suggest to them that they are very ill indeed. Their family and friends sometimes want them shielded from it in case they become frightened! But the sacraments are not insurances for death—they are assurances of life, for the life of the whole person. They are not reserved for the use of the dying. Even if the sick person is frightened, here is the very sacrament which casts out fear. Here in the sacrament are to be found not only the healing virtue of thanksgiving but also the peace that passes all understanding and allays our anxieties and fears. Here, too, we can offer up to God our very helplessness, our pain and depression.

I hope you haven't said you would prefer to wait until you are well enough to have it in your own church. It is in the sacrament of Holy Communion that Christ comes to 'make you better'. 'In truth,' he said, 'in very truth I tell you, unless you eat the flesh of the Son of Man and drink his blood you can have no life in you' (John 6.53).

There are some who feel they are not good enough. It is quite true, of course, that none of us is, but Christ 'did not come to invite virtuous people, but sinners'. His invitation is addressed not to those who think they are good enough but to those 'who truly and earnestly repent'. In spite of all your daily sins and failings, you can still come trusting in his manifold and great mercies. Though you may not be worthy to gather up the crumbs under his table, yet he is the same Lord whose property is ever to have mercy. In one of her letters a spiritual writer (Evelyn Underhill) reminds us that 'our Lord did not say, "Come unto me all ye faultless"; neither did he say, "Be sure you tear yourselves to pieces first". There are only three necessities of a good communion—faith, hope and charity. To rely utterly on God and be in charity with the world—this is the essential. What you happen to be feeling at the moment, does not matter in the least.'

You may not have received Holy Communion in hospital before and so feel rather sensitive about being on your own in the ward or in your side room. Even though you may be the only communicant you won't be actually receiving on your own. The very word 'communion' means 'fellowship', and you will be coming into the fellowship of the whole Church—militant, expectant, triumphant. It won't be 'my communion' but 'our communion'—our fellowship not only with Christ but with each other. Other patients in various wards throughout the hospital will also be partaking of the sacrament. Many, too, at the time will be present at the altars of churches of the parishes around you. You will therefore be sharing in communion with them just as surely as if you were kneeling alongside them, for in this sacrament you are united not only with your own parish church but with the whole body of Christ. Arrangements can be made for your family or members of the ward staff to receive their communion with you at your bedside.

And so we come: O draw us to thy feet,
  Most patient Saviour, who canst love us still;
And by this food, so awful and so sweet,
Deliver us from every touch of ill:
In thine own service make us glad and free,
  And grant us never more to part with thee.

AMR, 397

The service itself will be very brief, and in all probability the priest will bring you the sacrament which has already been consecrated at a service either in church or the hospital chapel, so that very few words are necessary at the bedside. This again helps you to realize that you are not cut off from the fellowship of the Church, but are sharing in the family worship still.

It may be that you are no longer a regular communicant. Perhaps you haven't made your Communion for a long time, and feel that it wouldn't be fair to ask for it now, having neglected it in the past! It isn't easy to begin again, I know, but here is a wonderful opportunity to accept his invitation again. Remember the words our Lord spoke at the Last Supper—'Take, eat: this is my body ... drink ye all of this, for this is my blood.' Those words have been echoed by the Church down the ages, and still in every Communion he gives us himself. You will be neglecting something which Christ, the Divine Physician, has most definitely provided for you. Please think about this, and remember the psalmist's words—'He healeth those that are broken in heart; and giveth medicine to heal their sickness.' Think of our Lord's command to you—'Do this in remembrance of me.' And of his invitation—'Come unto me all ye that labour and are heavy-laden and I will refresh you.' He is calling you to this holy sacrament. He did not say, 'Be worthy first and then come and do this.' No, his command is as unqualified as his invitation, and is as definite as his assertion, 'I come not to call the righteous but sinners to repentance.'

> Just as I am, though tossed about
> With many a conflict, many a doubt,
> Fightings and fears within, without,
>   O Lamb of God, I come.

AMR, 349

You will of course need to prepare yourself. The more trouble you take over your preparation the more the sacrament will mean to you. You just see how you are feeling and what your condition will allow. If you are too weak to make much effort then our Lord will perfectly understand. He knows just how you feel, and how difficult it is in sickness to fix one's thoughts for long on any kind of devotion. All he wants is your best under the circumstances, and he will accept it.

In Holy Communion Jesus gives you his very life. You ought, therefore, as far as your sickness allows, to give him thanks for such a great and wonderful gift. If you have a Eucharist book, and you feel well enough, you may like to read the collect, epistle, and gospel of the day, before the priest brings you the sacrament. You may also wish to think about some of the sayings of Jesus—'I am the bread of life' (John 6.35); 'This is my body: This is my blood' (Matt. 26.26). As you receive his body and blood you renew and strengthen your union with Christ in his death and resurrection, so picture our Lord on the cross, and recall the glory of the resurrection, with his promise: 'Lo, I am with you always.' Try to be as quiet as you can for a few minutes beforehand and think over the things you may have done wrong, or might have done better. Tell God about them quite simply in your own words, and be truly sorry for them. Then say: 'Help me, O God, to know my sins and to be truly sorry for them.' 'Make me a clean heart, O God: and renew a right spirit within me.' Remember God's readiness to forgive, and to strengthen us. Say: 'Lord I believe, help thou my unbelief.' 'O Saviour of the world, who by thy cross and precious blood hast redeemed me, save me and help me, I humbly beseech thee, O Lord'.

Be thankful. Holy Communion is, as one of its names, the Eucharist, implies, a service of thanksgiving, and you should approach it with a thankful heart. Say thankfully, 'I will give thanks unto thee, O Lord, with my whole heart'; 'Thanks be to God for his unspeakable gift'. Then finally be loving. Drive out any unkind or hard thoughts about others—be in 'charity with all men'. 'O come to my heart, Lord Jesus, there is room in my heart for thee.'

After the blessing when the priest has left you, you can thank our Lord for his gift and his love. Here are some suggestions which may help you with your thanksgiving:

Jesus my Lord, I thee adore, O make me love thee more and more.

God the Father, who made me, I thank you;

God the Son, who died and rose again for me, I thank you.

God the Holy Spirit, who makes me holy, I thank you.

It may be that you have not been confirmed and have been thinking over the years about this omission. It is never too late. If you wish to go forward and be confirmed your parish priest will be only too pleased to prepare you, and make arrangements for the bishop to come to your bedside and give you the strengthening gift of the Holy Spirit through the laying on of hands. You will then have the joy of communion with your Lord in the sacrament of his body and his blood.

The last receiving of the Holy Communion is normally called the 'Viaticum'—the food for the way indicating the continuing care of the Church for the dying. It will be our provision for the last journey—a journey that may not be so long as is commonly supposed. It will be the last of our Communions before the start of the journey into the life in which there will be no more need of sacraments.

The Sacraments 2

There's another sacrament I'd like to remind you about, particularly as it's one which is much misunderstood and one which has been rather neglected. It's the sacrament of Holy Unction, or anointing with oil. Some people seem to think it's only used in the Roman Catholic Church, or that it's a sacrament reserved for the dying. Both of these ideas are incorrect. It is becoming more and more frequently used within the Anglican Church, and it is administered for the healing of the sick and not solely for the comfort of the dying. It is the Church's great healing sacrament, and much grace and blessing follow its administration.

As I explained to you in a previous talk, the sacraments are outward and visible signs of an inward and spiritual grace through which God expresses himself and shows us his love. The outward and visible signs express most clearly the grace he gives us through them—water, the sign of cleansing, when we are baptized; bread and wine, the signs of nourishing, when we receive Holy Communion; and oil, the sign of healing, when we are anointed.

The Anglican Church recognizes Holy Unction as one of the lesser sacraments and it is normally administered to those who are leading a sacramental life, although its use is in no way restrictive. When a patient is unconscious he can still be anointed. We read about anointing with oil in Mark 6.13, where the twelve disciples told our Lord how they 'drove out many devils, and many sick people they anointed with oil and cured', and again in the Epistle of St James (5.13–16): 'Is any one among you suffering? Let him pray. Is any cheerful? Let him sing praise. Is any among you sick? Let him call for the elders of the church, and let them pray over him, anointing him with oil in the name of the Lord; and the prayer of faith will save the sick man, and the Lord will raise him up; and if he has committed sins, he will be forgiven. Therefore confess your sins to one another, and pray for one another, that you may be healed.' Such words are full of comfort and assurance. They imply that the sick are to place themselves entirely in God's hands to do with them and in them as he sees best. As with the other sacraments there's nothing magical about anointing. The very name 'Jesus Christ' signifies 'Jesus, the anointed one'. Oil too is used in the Coronation Service. When the present Queen was crowned in Westminster Abbey the Archbishop of Canterbury made the sign of the cross with oil on her forehead. It is a sacrament therefore not only of healing but of hallowing. It gives us healing and hallowing grace to withstand the many evil influences which prove such a great strain and create such stress to body, mind, and spirit in times of sickness.

> Father-like he tends and spares us,
> Well our feeble frame he knows,
> In his hands he gently bears us,
> Rescues us from all our foes,
> AMR, 365

as the hymn puts it.

The oil which is used is pure olive oil and it has normally been blessed by the bishop in his cathedral each Maundy Thursday. The short service at your bedside will normally begin with an antiphon—'O Saviour of the world, who by the cross and precious blood hast redeemed us; save us and help us, we humbly beseech thee O Lord.' There will be a brief psalm, lesson, confession of sin and absolution, and the Lord's Prayer. The priest will dip his thumb in the oil and anoint you on the forehead in the form of a cross, saying:

> Outwardly and with sacramental oil
> Your body has received anointing.
> So may Almighty God, our Father,

Inwardly anoint your soul, to strengthen you
With all the comfort and the joy
Of his most Holy Spirit.

Through the power of Jesus Christ our Lord
May you be loosed from all that troubles you
In body, mind, or spirit;
To praise the Blessed Trinity,
One God, beyond all time and space
Eternally, Amen.

The service is then brought to a conclusion with thanks-giving and blessing. I'm sure that the priest will use his dis-cretion as to the length of the service and be quite flex-ible about its official form.

The laying-on of hands used in conjunction with the anointing will represent the hands of the whole Church laid upon your head in his name, extending to you its com-passion and its love and concern. It will demonstrate the Church's commitment as a caring and healing community. It will be an acknowledgement of brotherly love and relationship, symbolizing the corporate unity of the whole body of Christ—our membership one of another. For this reason it is always helpful if your family can be at your bedside with you sharing in the sacrament and supporting the priest and yourself by their presence and their prayers. The prayer of the Church as well as the good will of your Christian friends will form a necessary part of the sacrament.

Your preparation for this sacrament is of course similar to that for the other sacraments. You may remember that I've already mentioned the importance of repentance—there should be either a formal or general confession if you are going to approach the sacrament in the proper frame of mind; of faith—a complete trust in God from whom comes 'all good living, every perfect gift' (James 1.17), and of charity—a concern for other sick people and a corporate and outgoing love for others. The sacraments are always potentially completely effective, but we can take advantage of them in some sense only as we try to fulfil these three conditions of penitence, faith, and charity—as far as your physical condition will allow, of course. The three are based upon relationships, when you think about them. Penitence is an attitude of mind towards God and other people. We can ask God to forgive us only if we ourselves are prepared to forgive others. Charity means being in a loving relationship not only with God but also with our fellow men. 'He that loveth not his brother whom he hath seen, how can he love God whom he hath not seen?'

Then faith—not expecting God to do what we ourselves want, but relating to God in perfect trust and being prepared to accept whatever may be God's will for us.

So much for preparation; what about results, you may well be asking? What is likely to happen if I am anointed? You need have no fear or doubt about 'whether it will work or not'. You can never put out your hand in faith to God without receiving some blessing. But what that particular blessing will be is not for us to demand or dictate. It may be physical, mental, or spiritual—sometimes all three. It must always be left entirely to God what the blessing will be. The benefits of the sacrament will almost certainly include the hallowing of the spirit, the quieting of the mind, and the allaying of fear and anxiety, enabling you to face up to your illness with renewed strength and inner calm. The definite feel of the holy oil, as the sign of the cross is made on your forehead, will inspire confidence and strengthen faith. The prime purpose of anointing is the strengthening of the soul rather than the mere physical improvement of the body, and we shall be pleased to leave the form of healing in the hands of God. The result is in his keeping and we must be prepared to trust him. We can never guarantee a cure but we can at least leave the end result in his hands.

Do have a word about the sacrament with the hospital chaplain or your own parish priest. He will be able to help and guide you and, should you desire the sacrament, will help you to prepare for it. The chaplain has already been visiting you, so feel perfectly free to express your feelings with him. You know that he will keep what you say in strictest confidence, and should you wish to be alone with him I'm sure your family and the ward staff will be pleased to arrange this. He often helps most by just being around—available and accessible whenever you need him. By his ministry he can bring you much comfort and support. Even if you have little or no faith, his mere presence with you may still bring you confidence and hope. He will try to come where you are, sharing your fears and problems with you and bringing you both courage and peace. Place every confidence in him, for he will not coerce or force you into a false profession of faith or compel you to receive the sacraments. There is no compulsion laid upon anyone to receive Holy Unction—or any of the other sacraments for that matter. Ask God's Holy Spirit to help guide you into a right decision. The very integrity of his love for you and companionship with you are all part of the Christian message. Yet it will be his duty to explain to you the means of grace and the strength and support you will derive from prayer and sacraments. He will do all he can to help you to realize the presence of God so that your pain can be used and your suffering transformed.

The chaplain will always be ready to give you a blessing, laying his hand upon your head and saying:

To God's gracious mercy and protection we commit you.
The Lord bless you and keep you.
The Lord make his face to shine upon you and be gracious unto you.
The Lord lift up the light of his countenance upon you, and give you peace.

He will also be able to grant you the precious gift of the

final blessing in the words of the wonderful commendatory prayer.

> Go further upon thy journey from this world, O Christian soul,
>
> In the name of God the Father Almighty who created thee.
>
> In the name of Jesus Christ who suffered for thee.
>
> In the name of the Holy Spirit who strengtheneth thee.
>
> In communion with the blessed Saints and aided by Angels and Archangels, and all the armies of the heavenly host.
>
> May thy portion this day be in peace, and thy dwelling in the heavenly Jerusalem.
>
> *Book of Common Prayer*, 1928

With your loneliness eased, your anxieties resolved, and your fears dispersed, upheld by faith in Christ and in the ministry of both word and sacrament, you can more readily surrender yourself to God with perfect calm and confidence.

Home or Hospital?

I hear that there is talk about your going home from hospital. You are going to discuss this with your family and make up your mind within the next few days. There is much to be said for being at home provided adequate care is available. If you know that you will be comfortable and have peace of mind, then home is the place. I'm glad the hospital has left the final choice with you and your family, for this is as it should be. If you finally make up your mind to return to your home you must be sure that the proper domiciliary support services are available in your area. This is very important for you must feel confident that you will have as skilled and efficient care in your home as you've been having when in hospital. Among your main needs will be a feeling of security, the control of your physical symptoms, and an assurance of companionship. Granted these, both you and your family can find a great sense of satisfaction and experience a feeling of achievement in being able to manage at home with the support and co-operation of the various community resources.

I'm sure you'll derive much emotional support from being constantly with your loved ones, in your own bed surrounded by all that is familiar—the furniture, the view, the garden, the neighbours, the natural surroundings. You will gain much too from the tender loving care of your loved ones. You feel so much more part of the family rather than part of a highly organized clinical environment of the hospital ward, no matter how skilled and thoughtful the nurses and other members of the staff are.

If you should find it difficult to make up your mind and can't make the final decision yourself then let someone who knows you very well help you to decide one way or the other—for example, a relative, one of your friends, your hospital or family doctor, the chaplain, or your own local clergyman. Probably the best guide will be your general practitioner after satisfying himself that home care is appropriate. Whoever helps you, there must be firm agreement between your family and yourself, assessing as fully as you all can the amount of work required and how best the various members of the family can adjust to the circumstances. Should your family feel at all anxious about having you home, fearing they might be inadequate or unable to cope, the doctor or the ward sister will be only too pleased to explain to them what will be needed and how best they can deal with various aspects of your illness. Much of their fears and apprehensions will then be resolved, and they will feel more adequate and secure when they know what medical and nursing support is available. They will see themselves as important members of the health-care team. One of the essentials of such care is that it is shared.

Unfortunately there is not always the liaison there should be between the hospital and the community. May I tell you about some of the more important links in the chain of communication. The prime members are the Community Nurse Co-ordinator, serving in liaison with those in the hospital, nursing, and medical social work teams, for these are the people who have all the relevant information about your present and future needs. Then there is the local health authority who will be providing the various facilities needed for your home care. There will also be your general practitioner, whom we have already talked about, and the various supporting services of social workers and voluntary services. All these should be working together as a team.

It will be ideal if one member of the caring team, the Community Nurse Co-ordinator or the health visitor for example, is prepared to act as a co-ordinator or supervisor in order to see that all the various services available within your area are alerted and your family kept continually in the picture. Trouble can easily arise if there is poor communication or the overlapping of services; wires become crossed and relationships strained, resulting in poor and inadequate teamwork and planning. The one person responsible can get all the wheels in motion, and assess the problems and needs.

It may be helpful to you and your family if I mention some of the persons who should be involved in caring for you at home and explain to you what their function is. There is of course your own home doctor who should be in constant touch with the hospital authorities. If he is one of a group practice or if there is a health clinic in your area, the health visitor, social worker, and community nurse will be attached to his team. Let's think of the health visitor. She'll help advise on your home care and act as liaison between the hospital and your general practitioner. She should be involved in preparatory plans for your homecoming and have already visited your family and discussed the necessary preparations with them. There will also be the community or district nurses who will be responsible for your nursing care. If necessary they will administer your pain-relieving drugs and whatever treatment the doctor prescribes for you. They will also be able to provide any special equipment you may need, e.g. a cradle to keep the bedclothes off your feet as you had in your hospital bed, back-rests, a rubber ring for you to sit on if an ordinary armchair is uncomfortable for you, rubber mats or drawsheets, commodes, bedpans, or urinals. You may need a feeding cup or a wool sheepskin. The use of sheepskins helps you to avoid pressure sores should you be confined to bed. The wool fibres are naturally springy and resilient, and retain these properties after washing. The woollen fibre mass tends to give as you change position in bed, and the sheepskin can be machine- or hand-washed and air- or spin-dried. Shaped woollen pads are also available for your heels and/or elbows. Should you be incontinent, special incontinence pads and polythene sheeting can be provided. In some areas there may be soiled laundry services available. The nurse can also show your family how best they can look after you and give them some useful practical hints—keeping a special eye on pressure areas; how best to lift you up should you slip down in bed; and seeing to the care of your mouth if necessary. She can perhaps arrange for your family or relatives to have a short break or a holiday should they at any time feel overtaxed or exhausted. She will also give them advice on any special diets and how best they can be prepared for you. Should there be any financial difficulties or emotional problems the social worker will be a most valuable member of the caring team. It might be possible to arrange for night-nurses if only on a part-time basis. The night-sitter service can relieve the members of your family should it be necessary for them to have to sit up with you by night. They can give you the necessary nourishment, adjust your pillows or your air-ring, and provide you with sedatives should they have been prescribed by your doctor. Arrangements might be made with the Social Service Department for a home help, as well as for the supportive assistance of social workers.

As well as the official services there are voluntary and non-medical amenities—The British Red Cross Society, the W.R.V.S. with their 'good companion' schemes and 'meals on wheels', the National Society for Cancer Relief (Michael Sobell House, 30 Dorset Square, London N.W.1), The Marie Curie Memorial Foundation (124 Sloane Street, London S.W.1), Invalids at Home (c/o 23 Farm Avenue, London N.W.2), the Good Neighbour Association (arranged locally). It is hoped that your local clergyman will be visiting you regularly if you belong to one of the churches in your area. As well as bringing you the sacraments should you desire them he can also be of moral support to the members of your family. He may also be able to arrange for persons in his congregation or belonging to one of the church organizations to help your family do the shopping, look after the children, babysit for them to have an evening out, help with the housework, prepare meals, and so on, without any intrusion into your family life or your own personal privacy. The hairdresser or beautician can also often serve as a grand morale-booster for you. The companionship of friends will serve to break the monotony of a long day or a restless night.

Your family should know that if it is necessary for any of your relatives to stay with you for six months or more they may be entitled to an Attendance Allowance grant. Forms for this are obtainable from the Post Office or Department of Health and Social Security. There are also special financial allowances available under the National Assistance Board. Naturally financial problems have to be considered, for quite possibly there will be extra expense in being at home—for example, extra heating may be needed, special diets, payment of home help, loss of wages of a member of your family. There are National Society for Cancer Relief grants, income tax relief, tax rebates, and Supplementary Benefits to offset these commitments, and I'm sure the social worker or your doctor will be able to help you with full particulars about these.

If you do decide to return home don't let the family spoil you too much. Let them see that you can still be a vital part of the family, sharing in its interests and involved in its decisions. You may even be able to participate in the everyday running of the house, in helping with the household chores, and in keeping the children amused, for example. Dependent upon how you feel, you can do some occupational therapy—perhaps paint, sew, make a cuddly toy or a lampshade, do some embroidery or fancy-work. You can also keep up some of your physiotherapy exercises which you learnt when in hospital. In all these various ways you can be yourself while at home and so continue to be an important member of the household and its management.

Whenever the need should arise, always remember that you can return to hospital—even if only for a short period of time. What we really need are some special units acting as halfway houses between hospital and home; there are so very few of them. Fortunately there are now more hospices being set up in various centres throughout the country. Many of these hospices are religious foundations, established as charities and working with the support of the Department of Health and Social Security. Some have teaching centres in which medical and nursing students and members of the caring professions gain experience on ward-rounds, in seminars and discussion groups, thereby playing an important role in present-day medical and nursing education. Other important advantages of such specialized units are that they are small, they create much local interest and concern, and the standard of nursing care is usually very high, being carried out with a deep sense of vocation and dedication. I've brought you along a list of them as well as of some of the Marie Curie Memorial Foundation Homes and Centres (see pp. 93–5).

All these services I've mentioned can help to improve the quality of life, for all who are involved in your care will be serving as a community to help express the fact that life goes on—ordinary continuing life—life of which sickness and death are only a part.

HOMES FOR TERMINAL AND LONG-TERM CARE

St Joseph's Hospice
Maré Street
Hackney
London E8 4SA

St Christopher's Hospice
51–3 Lawrie Park Road
Sydenham
London SE26 6DZ

Hostel of God
29–32 North Side
Clapham Common
London SW4

St Columba's Hospital
The Elms
Spaniards Road
London NW3 7JD

Hereford Lodge
Hereford Road
Bayswater
London W2

The Tarner Home
Tilbury Place
Brighton BN2 2GY

St Luke's Nursing Home
Little Common Lane
Off Abbey Lane
Sheffield S11 9HE

The Lady Cynthia Spencer House
Northampton

Copper Cliff Nursing Home
74 Redhill Drive
Brighton BH1 5 FL

Michael Sobell House
The Churchill Hospital
Headington
Oxford

The Douglas Macmillan Home
Barlaston Road
Blurton
Stoke-on-Trent
Staffordshire ST3 3NZ

St Joseph's Hospice Association
(Jospice)
Metropolitan Cathedral Buildings
Brownlow Hill
Liverpool L3 6 RQ

St Ann's Hospice
St Ann's Road North
Heald Green
Cheadle
Cheshire

St Margaret's Hospice
(Irish Sisters of Charity)
East Barn Street
Clydebank
Glasgow

St Barnabas' Home
Columbia Drive
Worthing BN13 2 QF

Horder Ward
The Royal Marsden Hospital
Fulham Road
London SW3

Our Lady's Hospice
(Irish Sisters of Charity)
PO Box 222
Harold's Cross
Dublin 6

Macmillan Unit
Christchurch Hospital
Christchurch
Hampshire

Jewish Home of Rest
Nightingale Lane
London SW12

The Marie Curie Memorial Foundation Homes and Centres

Ardenlea
Ilkley
Yorkshire

Holme Tower
Penarth
Glamorgan

Beaconsfield
Belfast

Strathclyde House
Glasgow

Conrad House
Newcastle upon Tyne

Sunnybank
Woolton
Liverpool

94

Fairmile
Edinburgh

Harestone
Caterham,
Surrey

Hill of Tarvit
Cupar
Fife

Tidcombe Hall
Tiverton
Devon

Warren Pearl House
Solihull
Warwickshire

The Children

What about the young children? How are they going to react if I finally decide to go home? Naturally I don't want them upset, and I've been thinking a lot about them since I came to hospital.

Well, fortunately they've been visiting you from time to time and I know they are looking forward to having you home with them. Children's attitudes to dying are extremely difficult to discover, for we adults know very little about how their minds work. In the past the tendency has been to keep all unpleasant and sad things from them.

What can I say about your own situation? I think it would be extremely difficult to exclude your children or grandchildren from some awareness of the severity of your illness. They needn't know all the facts but they should be allowed to share in the family's concern. It's a complete myth—the idea that what children don't actually see or hear they won't know, and that it's right to deceive them for their own good. Again the belief that children are 'too young to understand' is a sentiment which is often expressed to explain two very common but contradictory approaches to life-and-death situations.

Young children are either regarded as unable to take in anything unpleasant which is happening around them, and are therefore allowed to witness adult emotions and interactions without being offered any feasible explanations, or they are thought to be far too sensitive and vulnerable so that the true facts of life must be carefully and discreetly concealed from them. Often such attitudes are reflections of our own inner needs rather than a realistic appreciation of the true feelings of our children. After all it's only when we adults ourselves try to master our own conflicting feelings in the face of adversity that we become more able to adopt helpful attitudes towards our young children.

Instead of true answers to their many questions we tend to offer children half-truths, hastily concocted, hoping they will drop the subject and so let us off the hook, as it were. It will be not just *what* you all say as a family that will count but *how* you will say it. Your children's main source of strength at this time will be the realization that sickness and death can be talked about quite openly and without fear. It will be wise to make clear to them that whatever happens there will always be some members of the family around to look after them, care for them, and love them. Children are particularly sensitive to a highly emotional climate and have a fairly shrewd awareness of things in general even if they don't understand them in particular. They overhear things that are being said or whispered and become suspicious and anxious when they sense differences in family routine. Any noticeable change in the life of the household can cause them much distress and insecurity. If they are not given some sort of explanation of it all which fits what they overhear or sense, their imaginations are apt to run wild. They are aware that something's happening but they are not quite sure what it all means. It is always better, therefore, to tell them about the likely prospects no matter how distressing they are; otherwise they will search for meanings themselves, for no child lives in an emotional vacuum. Obviously such explanations will be modified by the age of your children or grandchildren and your understanding of their feelings. You will find, I'm sure, that they can face up to the truth far better than to deceit. The telling of the situation need not be at all formal and you shouldn't be over-anxious about it. Take things as they come—the more honesty that can be achieved in family discussions the better. They'll be able to grasp reality without any official explanation. Illness is a family crisis and they should be allowed to share in it and shown they have a part to play in it. As parents we can face up to questions from our children about the beginning of life far more easily than queries about the end of life—because we generally know all the answers!

Try if you can as a family to see what really is on your children's minds. Let them feel free to express whatever emotions may be welling up inside their little minds. Such sharing of emotions can be of great significance and you'll find it will bring your children a sense of fulfilment and dignity. Let them see there are things they can do and ways (no matter how small) in which they are needed. They understand much more than we adults usually realize. Make sure therefore you know what the children have in mind before any member of your family attempts to answer their questions, otherwise he or she will be answering questions which have not actually been asked. The explanation must be in words the children understand and expressed with all openness and honesty. They will feel much safer being included than being excluded. Honest answers are always preferable to dishonest evasions, for children respond to sincerity far more readily than falsehood. Should, however, there be moments when the family or yourself become particularly distraught or upset, very young children should if possible be spared being with you at such times.

The way in which your present circumstances are presented to your children or grandchildren will be of great importance for their whole future attitudes to dying and death. Children in general are surprisingly good at handling such situations—they are tough and resilient and able to cope—so long as they know they are being told the truth, and are being loved and cared for. At this time more than ever will it be necessary to say to each other, 'We need you and you need us. We are feeling just as you are feeling at this time.' In this way you can close the ranks and so make life as normal and stable as possible. Unless there are very special circumstances don't send the children off to relations to care for them. They'll be far more secure at home; if they're with other people—even if they are uncles or aunts—you'll find that it will only serve to heighten their sense of isolation and exclusion. They might also grow up to see sickness as something secretive and fearful.

Watch for any change in their behaviour, no matter how small the change may be. They may feel resentful that Mum is spending less and less time with them. Their anxiety is lessened if they know what's happening around them, as I've said. They may feel insecure, and insecurity may arouse in them anger and resentment. They may have feelings of guilt (I'd like to say more about this later). There may be sorrow at the thought of loss, anger at what's going on, and anxiety about the future; all this may have an effect on their behaviour. Such reactions and variations in behaviour will of course be very dependent upon the age and emotional make-up of the children. Very young children seem to deny the unpleasant, for the meaning of dying and death is grasped only by degrees. When they are aware of the situation they may feel most keenly the thought of separation. I should like to stress again that they can take truth but they cannot easily take deception or what seems to them to be deception. It has been said that children seem to have built-in lie detectors and I'm certain that's true. Questions should therefore be answered without evasion and on the level of their understanding—how much you think they can take. What you and your family know you can give honestly and consistently and—very important—as far as you are able, —follow it through with all possible support and guidance. Let the children know you understand their feelings at this time and give them full opportunity to talk about them if they wish to.

I'm afraid I don't know the ages of your children or grandchildren so may I explain to you how youngsters of various ages normally react to circumstances such as yours. Usually pre-school children cannot understand a great deal about dying and death. They may know that a member of the family has been away from home for a period of time and their rather vague emotions are likely to have few overtones. They have little concept of time: life is very much in the present and is largely made up of feelings. There is very little understanding of either time or distance. Rather than any formal attempt at explanation at this age, what is needed more is a warm and reassuring response of tender love and care. They will need interest shown in them—read them stories if you can, play games with them, help them with their jig-saws, watch the television with them—so that life goes on very much the same as usual.

Should the children be within the five-to-eight years range they will have a firmer grasp of things. They think a great deal. Those aged five tend to be calm and matter-of-fact about many things, including sickness. Their emotional world will be growing and they'll have more appreciation of time and distance. At the age of six most children are developing a strong and emotional phase, made evident by their temper tantrums. When they have their naughty spasms they may have feelings of guilt afterwards, and wonder whether what they've said has been the cause of the illness. They'll feel responsible for events in some way, and may need a lot of help to cope with these fears and anxieties within them—the reassurance that they are not responsible. They may want to work out their guilt feelings by deliberately misbehaving so that they can be reprimanded or punished.

When they reach the age of seven many children are likely to be calmer, and their idea of dying and death somewhat clearer. They may be curious about the causes of your illness and why you are sick. They may even begin to suspect that one day they too may be in similar circumstances. Death anxiety does occur in some children at a very early age, although it is in the sense of separation rather than of what we adults know as death. Children aged eight are typically less morbid and rather more expansive. They may wonder what happens when people die and where they go afterwards. Fantasies mingle with facts.

At nine most are ready to come to terms with life and death. Death is now being seen as the inevitable end of life, and from the age of eleven or twelve years they can enter into other peoples' feelings and talk freely about their own. They are usually able to share anxiety and concerns with understanding and a desire to be as helpful in the circumstances as they can. As regards adolescents it is extremely difficult to know what goes on in their minds regarding dying and death. To them abstractions often seem far more important than realities. It is an age for searching for meanings and values. They are apt to talk to friends and other adults at a deeper level than to their own parents about their feelings and experiences. They see themselves as adults and want others to see them as such as well. They should be given responsibility, for they are probably anxious to prove their identity and will acquire a sense of fulfilment if involved fully in the family's concerns at this time. Dying and death take on a religious significance and will form part of their search for the meaning of life and death. They sense they have a part to play, a right to belong, and will often emerge from the experience enriched and unharmed.

You'll appreciate, I know, that there can be no neat, clear-cut classifications describing the reactions of young children to dying and death. Each child is unique, and no two children will behave in an identical pattern. What I've tried to outline for you must be understood in very general terms. You'll know your children or grandchildren far better than anyone else; each will be an individual in his own right and must be given every opportunity to express himself in his own way.

It may also be helpful to know that young children are often taken aback when they first see their parents cry—particularly if father cries. It somehow shatters the image they may have of adulthood. It may also be due to the fact that parents themselves had previously scolded them for crying under different circumstances or told them to stop crying when being naughty—'Do stop crying.' 'Don't cry; be a man!' 'Only babies cry!' The importance of tears and the feelings which go with them during a family crisis should be explained, so that the children don't feel emotionally rejected or injured. It can be told them that to cry is but a natural and normal expression of feeling.

Preparing children to think and talk freely about dying and death is the duty of every Christian parent. If such instruction forms part of the normal upbringing of children then they are more equipped to deal with death when it occurs in the family circle. It is important that when death is explained to children it should be done in terms that are not only religiously valid but also emotionally satisfying to them. Words uttered at such a critical time will live long in their memories, and they quickly sense the sincerity or otherwise of what is said during highly emotional periods. Sadly, some of the more common expressions used by some parents are not as helpful and satisfying as they might be. Indeed I would go so far as to say that many are positively harmful. 'Jesus is taking Grandma away from us.' 'God wants to take her to heaven.' Even when the family have strong religious affiliations, the terms in which they express death to their children can become far too abstract and can represent to the mind of a child a rather cruel, avengeful, horrid sort of 'God' who wants to take his Grandma away from him. What young children want is not so much a mere theory or explanation of death, but far more important a sense of reassurance and sustaining security.

The questions they want to ask are in the main simple and straightforward and often have to do with the physical aspects of death. What happens when people die? Are their eyes open or closed? Why are they put in a deep hole in the ground? Will I die one day? Does everyone have to die? Many children have seen pictures of funerals, and victims of earthquakes, floods, and starvation on television programmes and will be familiar with seeing death portrayed in 'Westerns' and other films. The questions they ask are their own particular way of showing their feelings and present an excellent opportunity to teach and prepare them for future crises. Much will depend upon their various ideas and thoughts of death and on any previous explanations you might have given when a family pet had died or been killed, or when they had found a dead bird in the garden and begun asking questions. The difficulty is of course that there are so many kinds of death, and children will differ in their reactions. If an elderly member of the family dies mother can explain simply that if the body is worn out then Grandma or Grandpa has no further use of it, and in heaven bodies will be no longer needed and Grandma or Grandpa will go on living without pain or trouble. You can also use illustrations from nature, explaining to them what happens throughout autumn and winter, and then new life appearing in spring and summer. The leaves from the trees wither and die and fall to the ground and then new life begins again when fresh buds form on the branches. There are the bulbs that you plant in the bowl at home, put away in the darkness and then later bring out into the light and sunshine and await their blooms.

I don't think it's as helpful as it sounds to refer to 'God's will' with young children, for this may so easily arouse in their minds an anger and rebellion against such a God and his cruel 'will'. They can get terribly frightened, dreading that the same 'will' may be the cause of their own deaths. Such fears can lead to nightmares and aggressive and delinquent behaviour. I wouldn't recommend relating death to sleep at this stage, either. There may again be fears than when the child himself goes to sleep or is put to bed he or she may never wake up again.

They can be told quite simply about the life to come where there will be no more pain or death, and where those who have died go on living in a different world and in a different form. Here will be the time for you all as a family to get right away from the fairy-tale act and get right down to the heart of the gospel. They will be constantly grateful to you in later life, for such instruction

103

will build up their confidence and help them to see death as part of human experience. Such a family crisis, if faced creatively, can be the means of enabling the children in your home to grow and to mature. Helping them to understand the truth will be of great benefit to you all. As a family you will have to search for simple yet straightforward language to help the children all you can. I feel confident that you'll all find renewed strength in facing reality together with truth as your guide. You will help them and your children will help you. Finally may I remind you that they must have something secure and stable to cling to at this time; they must also have something truthful to believe in. Granted this, then whatever their ages may be, they will derive from their present experience a deeper understanding of death and a stronger faith in the life hereafter.

TALK SIXTEEN
Grief

When you know you have to leave behind those who are near and dear to you, and those who have formed part of your life for many years, it is but natural for you to feel keenly the painful pangs of grief. Our talks together would be incomplete if we didn't think about this subject of grief, and try to understand a little more about it. In grief we search for answers, but there are no answers—no satisfactory ones at any rate. Why do we have these intense feelings? Well, first we grieve for ourselves—our sense of loss at the thought of being separated from our loved ones. We are naturally sad because we are being deprived of their love and companionship. Second, there is fear. We don't know how our family and dependents will fare without us. There's also the fear of the unknown—the unrevealed future.

Grief is the price we have to pay for love, and both you and your family will be experiencing somewhat similar emotions. It will be helpful therefore if your anguish of grief can be shared together. I know that not all families will feel up to doing this, but if it is at all possible for you, you'll find that in this sharing much of your fear and anxiety, and feelings of bitterness and loneliness, will be lessened and your deepest thoughts given full expression. As we've said before, family members often suffer if they can't express their grief and share it with you. You can't avoid the pain of parting but at least you can work through it together. Grief is an intense emotion and to bottle it up will only lead to trouble later on, for it brings with it a flood of negative feelings. When Jesus informed his disciples of his impending death he was aware of the *sorrow* that filled their hearts. Even with the knowledge of reunion parting brings sorrow. Even in the light of the resurrection it brings a sadness which is real and completely consistent with our Christian faith. Our faith doesn't preclude grief nor the need for working through it. You can well imagine the gnawing feelings of *loneliness* and *isolation* which Mary Magdalene and the other women went through when they rushed to the sepulchre on the first Easter morning. 'On the Sunday morning very early they came to the tomb bringing the spices they had prepared. Finding that the stone had been rolled away from the tomb, they went inside; but the body was not to be found ... they stood *utterly at a loss* ...'(Luke 24.1–3). Feelings of *frustration* filled the minds of the two disciples on the road to Emmaus in the evening of that same Easter Day, when they grieved over the losing of their long-awaited Messiah. 'That same day two of them were on their way to a village called Emmaus, which lay about seven miles from Jerusalem, and they were talking together about all these happenings. As they talked and discussed it with one another, Jesus himself came up and walked along with them; but something held their eyes from seeing who it was. He asked them, "What is it you are debating as you walk?" They halted, their faces *full of gloom* ...' (Luke 24.13–17). You will remember too Peter's feelings of *guilt* and his *tears* of *remorse*: 'At that moment the cock crew. And Peter remembered how Jesus had said, "Before the cock crows you will disown me three times." He went outside, and wept bitterly' (Matt. 26.75); the *anger* of Thomas: 'Unless I see the mark of the nails on his hands, unless I put my finger into the place where the nails were, and my hand into his side, I will not believe it' (John 20.25); the *fear* of all Jesus' followers who forsook him and fled in hiding: 'The disciples all deserted him and ran away' (Matt. 26.56). All these are common reactions to grief, and what the disciples and his followers experienced when they were losing Jesus through death are exactly the same emotions which we all go through under similar circumstances today.

I've used these illustrations from the Gospels to help

you see that there's nothing irreligious about giving vent to grief. You'll find that the closer your relationships are with those around you the more intense your symptoms of grief will be. Never be ashamed of your emotions, and don't think for one moment that they're a sign of weakness or due to a lack of faith on your part. Be free to express as much grief as you feel—no more, no less. The verses I have just been reading to you don't imply, of course, that you and your family will go through all these different reactions nor necessarily experience them in the order in which I have mentioned them. What these examples from Scripture do mean is that you can be quite sure that your feelings at this time of grief and loss are very normal and very natural. It's most important for you to remember that. It's rather difficult to differentiate clearly between them, for no one moves neatly out of one and into the other, and of course we all have different temperaments.

Shall we now consider some of the signs and symptoms of grief a little more fully? Among the most common of such feelings will be loneliness and bewilderment. Your whole life-pattern is being disrupted and broken. There will be the feeling of loss—loss not only in terms of the severing of relationships, but also the loss of health and strength; loss of the role you once played in the home and the community; loss of the sense of belonging. The seeming emptiness and change that have come over you are painful experiences to bear. The ache is deep and sense of loss acute. Another characteristic is fear—fear of death itself, and the fear of what pain and suffering your death will cause your loved ones. You may often feel angry and bitter, becoming critical of everything and everybody. We are apt to take such circumstances personally, as it were, seeing them as something done to us, and so we seek for someone to blame. There will be moments of utter depression and you may find yourself thinking thoughts you seldom have under more normal circumstances. You may feel God doesn't care any longer and you may even doubt that he exists. It becomes difficult to concentrate, and your mind may be full of unpleasant thoughts. Closely related to depression are feelings of guilt. You begin to think of all the things you should have done differently: it is as if you have to punish yourself with total dejection and unhappiness. You are inclined to judge yourself harshly and feel that your life has fallen far below a standard of fulfilment. You express self-disappointment: 'Why didn't I . . . !' You preoccupy yourself with the past, and all the 'shoulds' of life seem to pass through your mind. The sins of omission loom up as large if not larger than the sins of commission. When you have such feelings of guilt, some of it is real and some is neurotic. It is to be expected that there will be real guilt, for no family can live in deep and close relationship without hurting each other from time to time. These unhappy experiences come rushing back to memory, and it is extremely difficult to work through such powerful emotions of guilt. Where there has been real guilt and evidence of neglect, forgiveness can be sought in the ways I described to you in a previous talk. It will do you no good to keep on brooding over the past. You become unhealthily introspective and morbid if you do. There's a piece of doggerel verse which sums up the situation rather well:

> Once in saintly passion
> I cried with desperate grief,
> 'O Lord, my heart is black with guile.
> Of sinners I am chief'.

> Then stooped my guardian angel
> And whispered from behind,
> 'Vanity, my little man,
> You're nothing of the kind'.
> Anon.

Tears are a safety valve God has given you to release your innermost emotional pressures; they are meant to relieve tension. You've already found that 'a good cry' can prove a power of help. There are some people who have been so conditioned in life that they exercise great control over their emotions. They do not easily become angered or upset: they never seem to be either extremely happy or very depressed. Others again are highly sensitive and emotional, and tears come very naturally. They are easily excitable with high pitches of emotional feeling. Each one of us is unique and will react differently from the other. What I would suggest is that you express as much sorrow as you feel—in the way which comes most naturally to you. When Lazarus, 'whom Jesus loved', died, Jesus himself wept. (In Moffatt's translation we read, 'He burst into tears.') When Mary learnt that they had taken away her Lord and she 'knew not where they had lain him' she, too, could not refrain from crying. Faith doesn't demand a stoical indifference to your feelings. Neither should you falsify your emotions in conformity with public convention. What you and I must resist if possible is the brooding grief which is full of self-pity, for this is the grieving 'as those without hope' (1 Thess. 4.13). There's a world of difference between self-pity when thoughts are centred on self, and genuine grief when hopes and thoughts are centred on God. Little help is promised to the former, for it is only the latter—those who grieve—who will be comforted (Matt. 5.4). The healing process of tears can wash away some of the poison and bitterness which may be lying dormant in your mind, so never be ashamed of shedding them. I remember reading that 'No doctor's medicine—no tender solicitous nursing, no strong tonic, has such a powerful effect on suffering humanity as the shedding of tears ... and above all remember that the tears shed for others are precious gifts that are as priceless in God's sight as frankincense and myrrh.' Grief will be a testing of your faith, for you will doubtless have moments of despair and unbelief—moments when you have to wrestle with God; when you will want to cry out, 'Lord I do believe but help thou my unbelief!' There will perhaps be days of defeat and gloom, but God knows and understands.

As well as darkness there will be light. There will be new perspectives if you look for them. The way through grief is to accept it as far as you are able—to work through its full anguish of loss by open expression, sharing it with those around you. I'm sure you'll derive much support from your family and friends, and much of you will live on in them. You will be the recipient of their love and affection, thereby lightening the sense of loss. Your faith, your courage, and your hope will be nurtured within the circle of your family and the caring community about you. Their warm affection and encouragement will strengthen your faith in the future and your will to live. If you are prepared to face up to things honestly and openly then you are on the first step towards overcoming them. Sorrow tends to become more and more painful through being kept secret. Grief can bring you a new understanding of yourself and your family—a discovering of the real 'you'; a deeper and richer sympathy for others. Your life can become more mature with the ability to adjust yourself to your present predicament. You will find much inner comfort if you can become master of your circumstances rather than allowing yourself to be mastered by them. If you can use your pain and sorrow creatively you can then let go of all illusions and cling to spiritual truths and so learn the positive power of a sustaining faith. Yours will then be a security unshaken by circumstance and there will be a sense of serenity in the midst of your sadness. Grief can be a way in which God enables you to grow through loss—your time of dying becomes your time of living; of receiving and giving meaning and joy in ways you've never experienced before. The natural threat of death is then transformed into a spiritual reality, for you will be possessed of values that death itself can never destroy.

Healing comes only by facing reality. God will guide the future as he has done the past. Who was it that said, 'We are healed of a suffering only by experiencing it to the full'? If you try to ignore this fact or pretend that it doesn't exist your whole life will become blunted and unfulfilled. I was reminded of the importance of this when re-reading *The Plague*—that great novel by Camus. There's a quotation from the book which brings home so well the very point I'm making:

> They forced themselves never to think, to cease looking to the future, and always to keep, so to speak, their eyes fixed on the ground at their feet. But naturally enough, this prudence, this habit of feigning with their predicament and refusing to put up a fight, was ill rewarded. For, while, averting that which they found so unbearable they also deprived themselves of redeeming moments, frequent enough when all is told. Thus, in a middle course between heights and depths, they drifted through life rather than lived, the prey of aimless days and sterile memories, like wandering shadows that could have acquired substance only by consenting to root themselves in the solid earth of their distress.

Help comes in grief through quiet confidence, faith, and hope. If you can find a meaning to life in spite of all that is now happening to you—a meaning which includes even suffering and death—this will sustain you at all times as you face the future. If you can say in the midst of the pain and sadness of grief, 'Still there is a meaning', you will derive a deep sense of growth, of fulfilment, of wholeness. You will find new strength and fresh potentials. There's a saying: 'He who has a *why* to live for can bear almost any *how*.' If you have something—or someone—to live for or to hope for you will be able to put up with this present painful 'how'. May God grant that this may be so.

TALK SEVENTEEN
Christian Death

How best can we understand the meaning and the significance of death? This to say the least is not an easy question to answer, but it has to be faced. I shall try to be as simple and straightforward as I can without, I hope, becoming too theological. The bedside of the sick is no place for lectures in theology as you must well appreciate.

Let's think about it this way first. Death is *natural*. Death is a universal law of nature. It's a law from which no living thing can possibly escape. I remember reading a story once about a governor of one of our overseas colonies who unfortunately had suffered a series of bereavements in his family during his term of office. Not only did his wife die but also two of his children. As a result he became determined to keep from his remaining children all knowledge of death. He retired to a secluded and beautiful island and there attempted to conceal from his daughters any thoughts of dying and death. Death became a forbidden word—it was not to be mentioned; neither was it to be anticipated. If a death did occur on the island the body was secretly removed and the children kept well away from the scene. No questions were asked, no answers were given. One can well imagine how such an experiment was doomed to failure from the start. Dead branches from the trees, the falling leaves, the fading flowers, the withering grass, fish lying on the coral reef, birds killed in the tropical forest all revealed to the daughters the very truths which were meant to be hidden. To them as to all of us, the time came when the presence of death, in spite of all attempts at concealment and denial, insisted on making itself known as a natural process of nature. Dust we are and to dust all of us have to return. We live to die. Man is 'mortal'—that is, 'one who dies'. In other words death is all part of the ongoing experience of life. It makes evolution and development possible. It prevents us 'continuing in one stay' and opens the gate to higher states of being. Death is certain—do what we will, go where we will, consult whom we may. In spite of all our wonderful achievements and miracles of medicine and surgery, our ultra-modern coronary care and intensive care units, the death rate always remains at 100 per cent. In our heart of hearts we may yearn for a life without death but our minds and our logic reject it. Remember the old legend of 'The Wandering Jew' who is said to have refused to help the dying Christ on the way to the crucifixion, and how he was therefore doomed never to die himself—a fate more terrible than any death! Life has death as its boundary and thereby it gives life its true meaning and value. Life after all should be seen as a time given us to respond freely to the purposes of God and so become 'children of God' and 'heirs of eternal life'. Having told you that death is natural I don't want you to overlook the fact that it is still 'the last enemy'. Neither do I want you to underestimate its ugliness and bitterness. You have only to look at the crucifix to have this brought home to you. Death after all is an intruder, an enemy, as the Bible tells us, so it would be quite wrong and misleading of me to sentimentalize it in any way. The real bitterness of death is to be found in its moral evil—'the sting of death is sin'—that pride which mars and spoils our true nature, created as we are in the image and likeness of God. Although death is the natural and expected end of life, this in no way implies that we all have to be enthusiastic about death. Even Jesus himself shrunk from it as you may remember from the Passion story I read to you during a recent talk. Few people really want to die. The majority of us want to go on living—not so much because our faith is weak, but because there's so much life— God's life—right here, in ourselves and in those we love. What I want to emphasize is that it's not *enthusiasm* so much as *readiness* which is all-important. Do you recall those wonderful words of Martin Luther King in what was to be his last sermon in Memphis, Tennessee: 'I would like to live a long life, but I have been to the mountain top and I have seen the promised land.' Death is natural because it's an inevitable end of this life; that's the first point I'd like you to remember.

The second is that death is *personal*. It's a unique personal reality in every man's life. My death may be reported as one more statistic but it is still uniquely my own. No one else can die for me. Our life is a gift and comes from God. We accept life from him—together with its joys and its sorrows—and we can in our prayers and actions offer it back to him. You hold your life and I hold mine as stewards, and we know that God will do with our lives and with ourselves whatever is right and good. In his good time and in his good way we can be confident that it will become clear to us that his way is the best way. When we are prepared to leave things in his hands then we share in his divine purpose both for ourselves and for the world. 'O God, I don't understand what is happening to me, but I leave everything confidently into your hands!'

Death is not so much something that happens to us as rather something we do. It's a sort of self-abandonment, a total giving up of ourselves, a complete emptying of ourselves. It's a 'Yes'—an 'I do'. It's an act that you and I personally have to perform—an act or sacrifice of thanksgiving for all that life has meant to us; it's a gift of which we are custodians. In death each of us has to render it back to God for his use. It is the only way in which we can personally give ourselves to God. In dying we give back to God all that we are and all that we have. Our life can then be given back to him renewed and immortalized, enriched, and empowered with his divine life. I wonder if you've read *The Lord of the Rings* by Tolkien. If so you'll probably remember Aragorn, the noble king approaching old age and realizing that the span of his lifedays is drawing to an end. He says to Arwen, his wife: 'At last, Lady Evenstar, fairest in this world and most beloved, my world is fading. Lo! We have gathered and we have spent, and now the time of payment draws near . . .' And he then adds this beautiful phrase: 'To me has been given, not only many years but also the grace to go at my will, and give back the gift.' Aragorn's words, 'giving back the gift', ring true for us all, for life is a gift.

> O Love that wilt not let me go,
>   I rest my weary soul in thee:
> I give thee back the life I owe,
> That in thine ocean depths its flow
>   May richer, fuller, be.
>
> AMR, 359

We can hand ourselves over wholly to God in loving trustfulness: 'Father, into thy hands I commend my spirit', adding, 'For thou hast redeemed me, O Lord, thou God of truth' (Ps. 31.6). So death becomes for the Christian a moment of completion—a total self-offering—a letting-go of self and a giving of oneself to God in love and utter confidence. Death then will become gain through loss. 'If we have died with Christ, we believe that we shall also live with him' (Rom. 6.8).

Third, death is *social* and *communal*. We are social beings and we can only discover our true meaning and identity in relationships with other people. Death takes place in a community and the community is involved. Each needs the other; those who are dying need the community to comfort, support, and be with them, and the community needs the dying to help them face the basic realities of life and ask important questions about life. Our very anxiety about death inevitably arises out of a love of life and a love of all the relationships within that life which have brought meaning and significance to it. The sting of death is the severing of these relationships. Death can never be a private matter. You probably know that well-quoted piece from John Donne: 'Any man's death diminishes me, for I am involved in mankind.' The Christian community can play its part in educating us for death. All human beings are valuable, lovable, of significance. If we have been loved and accepted by others and we in turn have shown unselfish service to others, then death will be easier for all of us to accept. Our whole life therefore in a Christian community can be a preparation for death. It can be seen as a transition from one relationship with God and our fellow men to another. If we see ourselves as living in the presence of God and sharing other relationships within the community, then we know that death comes not as a final tragedy or separation but simply as another episode in life, to be faced with confidence in the ultimate outcome: 'Whatever happens—whether I get well or not—everything will be all right.'

We have spoken together a great deal about the importance of the family and how essential their support is at this time. We have also discussed the pros and cons of being at home or in hospital. May I ask you and those dear to you to make dying a family experience if you possibly can—whether you remain in hospital or return home. In an atmosphere of personal sensitivity towards each member of the family, love for each other, a sense of genuine relationship with each other, death can then be faced more and more as a community and family event. Good-byes can be said together, and dying becomes a moving and meaningful experience for all concerned. In this way not only what remains of your life but also the lives of the community around you will be enriched, the last phase of life looked upon not as defeat but rather as a fulfilment of all that has gone before. Death will no longer be seen as the worst thing that can happen, and each day will be seen less and less as an accepted period of time, and more and more as something most precious and sacred.

Finally, death is *mysterious*; the greatest of all mysteries, most final of all finalities. 'Time like an ever rolling stream bears all its sons away.' Your friends and family can say to you, 'We want to understand', 'We are anxious to share your burden', but no one can talk about dying and death from experience. It's beyond our knowing, and so immediately we are beset by limitations. To many of the other experiences of life we can say: 'I know what it's like—I've been through it myself!' 'I can speak from experience.' But here we are all up against the unknowable. If you ask me, 'What exactly is death?' I should find it very difficult to answer, for nobody knows what it actually is. I can have theories about it; I can witness the effects of it; but these things would bring me no nearer to understanding what it really is. Perhaps the nearest we can get to it is in the clear and precise words of the Psalmist (104.29)—'When thou taketh away their breath they die.' The Bible tells us very little about death, except that it is a reality all of us have to face. Jesus himself in both his teaching and his preaching does not mention a great deal about death—what he emphasized was the importance of life. The New Testament seems far more concerned with daily living than with bedside dying. Its one specific for a good death is a good life.

Yet death can never be seen as a total loss or inexplicable mystery if seen as the final offering of our life to God. We have the strong assurance that 'He leads us through no darker rooms than he went through before'. He will never leave us or forsake us. Christian death is at once both like and unlike any other forms of death. It is like them physically, of course. The Christian's body decays and dies like that of other men, yet they who, like Simeon, have seen the Lord Christ can pray in all sincerity and right good hope: 'Lord, now lettest thou thy servant depart in peace, for mine eyes have seen thy salvation.' Whatever be the manner of dying, when all is finished they can humbly, yet confidently, repeat the last words of their crucified Lord: 'Father, into thy hands I commend my spirit.' But whereas Christian deaths are physically like the deaths of other men, in every other respect they are greatly unlike. What the world calls death is not death to the Christian. Death cannot be death if it raises us in a moment from darkness into light, from weakness into strength, from sinfulness into holiness. Death cannot be death if it brings us nearer to Christ who is the fount of life. Death cannot be death; for Christ has conquered death for himself, and for those who trust in him. For the Christian death is a fresh start. It is not a leap into the dark; it is the opening of and entrance into the floodgates of light. Do you remember the collect for Easter Eve? I'll read it to you, for it speaks of death as a 'gate': 'Grant, O Lord, that as we are baptised into the death of thy blessed son our Saviour Jesus Christ, so by continual mortifying our corrupt affections we may be buried with him; and that through the grave, and gate of death, we may pass to our joyful resurrection; for his merits, who died, and was buried, and rose again for us, thy son Jesus Christ our Lord.' You can think of death as a chancel gate, as it were, opening the way into the very sanctuary of God's presence. By dying Christ opened that gate for us, that where he is there we might be.

For the Christian the moment of death is not only the moment of truth but also the moment of glorious, triumphant hope.

> Still let me prove thy perfect will
> My acts of faith and love repeat;
> Till death thy endless mercies seal,
> And make the sacrifice complete.
> AMR, 329

It is in the two great sacraments of baptism and the Eucharist whereby the Christian participates sacramentally in the dying and rising of Jesus, that death can be most clearly understood. In baptism the ownership of our bodies, so to speak, changed: we now live in the person of Christ, who is the Resurrection and the Life. To perfect the work of baptism we have the Eucharist. 'He who eats my flesh and drinks my blood has eternal life, and I will raise him up at the last day' (John 6.5.). Death becomes our final opportunity to share totally the life of

Christ. The process begun in baptism and fulfilled in the Eucharist reaches its full circle. Death is the final door for us. Death changes its whole aspect when seen through Christ, yet we mustn't become depressed should we find our reactions not what we had hoped or our faith as strong as we might want. What really matters will be our whole life and its trend and becoming, not just what may be our feelings at this time of physical discomfort and weakness. God is 'full of compassion and mercy: long-suffering, plenteous in goodness and truth'. Ponder through the verses of that psalm (86) if you can. They are so wonderfully filled with the assurance of his love that you can rest on it in faith, letting nothing disturb you. I think the best practical advice I can give you should such doubts or fears be worrying you is to trust God and give yourself to him. His way of leading you may not be his way of leading some other person, for we are all so very different. Just be content to let him lead you in his own way specially for you. Perhaps it may help if I tell you a story about an incident which happened during the recent bombing in Northern Ireland. A bomb had blown up a large store in the centre of a city. It was crowded with shoppers, among whom were a father and his small son. Fortunately the father ran for safety under cover and urged the youngster to jump down to be with him. Hearing his father's voice encouraging him to jump, the small boy exclaimed: 'I can't! I can't see you.' To which, stretching out his arms, the father replied, as he saw his son anxious, fearful, and bewildered: 'But *I* can see *you*. Jump!' So the faith which you need to face death is the assurance not so much that you can see but that you are seen; not that you know but that you are known.

Dying is the last chapter of life, and as you well know a last chapter can be the most crucial, the most inspiring and exciting, the most challenging of all. Your last hour can bring out the best of you and bring a perfect completion to your life. It can be a victory. I pray that you will find reconciliation and peace, that you will continue to grow until your last moments, and that you will hear Christ saying to you: 'It is I, be not afraid.' May your last hour be your finest hour, so that 'dying, behold you live'.

TALK EIGHTEEN
Christian Hope

Is there a life after death? If so, what will it be like? Will I meet my loved ones again? These are very natural questions which we must now consider together. Let's take them in order. Will there be an afterlife? The scepticism of Thomas is unfortunately re-echoed in the minds of many people today: 'The disciples told him, "We have seen the Lord." He said, "Unless I see the mark of the nails on his hands, unless I put my finger into the place where the nails were, and my hand into his side, I will not believe it"' (John 20.25). They want 'signs and wonders' before they are prepared to believe. They demand scientific proof—the Q.E.D. of a mathematical problem. Now I can't of course supply you with these, but what I can say is that as Christians we are provided with three very good reasons for belief in the life hereafter. I'll try to summarize them briefly for you.

First of all we have our Lord's own *belief* in immortality. The conviction of a life after death formed the background of his whole life—it permeated his precepts and his parables and was the ultimate basis of all his teaching. You remember his last words from the cross: 'Father, into thy hands I commend my spirit' (Luke 23.46). They are representative of his lifelong conviction that life persists through death. Then we have his *teaching* on life after death. 'He that believeth in me,' he has promised, 'though he were dead, yet shall he live: And whosoever liveth and believeth in me shall never die' (John 11.25–6). He told his disciples, 'I go now to prepare a place for you. And if I go and prepare a place for you, I will come again, and receive you unto myself, that where I am, there ye may be also' (John 14.2–3). He comforted the dying thief on the cross with solemn assurance: 'Verily, I say unto thee, today thou shalt be with me in paradise' (Luke 23.43).

It is therefore unthinkable for the Christian to believe that death ends all. Third and most important of all we have our Lord's own *experience*. 'He both died and rose.' The story of the empty tomb is related in all the four Gospels. Shall I read to you the account from St Matthew's Gospel (28.5–7): 'The angel then addressed the women [Mary of Magdala and the other Mary]: 'You', he said, 'have nothing to fear. I know you are looking for Jesus who was crucified. He is not here; he has been raised again, as he said he would be. Come and see the place where he was laid, and then go quickly and tell his disciples: "He has been raised from the dead and is going on before you into Galilee; there you will see him.' That is what I had to tell you."'

Christ's resurrection is the warrant of our own. 'Because I live,' he promised us, 'ye shall live also.' What happened to Christ is the guarantee of what is to happen to those who believe in and follow him. 'For, the truth is, Christ was raised to life—the first-fruits of the harvest of the dead. For since it was a man who brought death into the world, a man also brought resurrection of the dead. As in Adam all men die, so in Christ all will be brought to life.' Christ's resurrection from the dead has destroyed the power of death and has given back to us everlasting life. 'Now if this is what we proclaim,' St Paul tells us, 'that Christ was raised from the dead, how can some of you say there is no resurrection of the dead? If there be no resurrection, then Christ was not raised; and if Christ was not raised, then our gospel is null and void, and so is your faith' (1 Cor. 15.12–14). He then adds a final point which seems to clinch his argument: 'If it is for this life only that Christ has given us hope, we of all men are most to be pitied' (v.19). Death for the Christian is a door not into a dark and foreboding unknown but into the presence of Christ. As death was not the end for Christ neither will it be for us. It would be incredible to think Christ would have died for us if the grave were the end. The question of Job—which is the question of so many today—'If a man die shall he live again?' can only be answered, not by the doubtful 'I hope' or the uncertain 'I think', but with those splendid words of confidence and conviction: 'Death is swallowed up in victory.'

What form will the resurrection take? you ask. St Paul describes it rather dramatically in 1 Corinthians. Let me read it to you: 'Lo, I tell you a mystery. We shall not all sleep, but we shall be changed, in a moment, in the twinkling of an eye, at the last trumpet. For the trumpet shall sound, and the dead shall be raised imperishable, and we shall be changed. For this perishable nature must put on the imperishable, and this mortal nature must put on immortality ... Then shall come to pass the saying that is written "Death is swallowed up in victory".' He goes on to tell us to look at the miracle of spring. The seed you sow in the garden or in the field is an ordinary seed; part of it decays and dies, and that which lives comes up as a green blade completely different in appearance from the seed originally sown. So God gives us a body which will be a fitting instrument for the new conditions of another world. It will be the same yet different, adapted for life under heavenly conditions. Our present bodies are 'terrestial', as St Paul says. They tie us to earth. Our future bodies will be 'celestial', adapted to the spiritual and eternal things in the midst of which our future life is to be passed. As we bear 'the image of the earthy', so we shall bear 'the image of the heavenly'.

I don't want you to imagine that death is a mere separation of soul and body, for the resurrection does not mean that our bodies will be raised to physical life after death. It is the whole person which rises in the resurrection— the whole person is raised to share in resurrection life. Our body is an essential part of our personality, and in death that body perishes but is not lost, for it is reconstituted in glory. It will be 'a spiritual body' which will be quite different from our present earthly body. In other words we shall not be in a sort of shadowy existence with disembodied spirits. We shall not be 'ghosts' or 'souls'.

We shall be ourselves. The resurrection will be a resurrection of our personality—that is our whole selves, recognizable yet spiritual. The real 'you' lives on. The clause in the creed which speaks of 'the resurrection of the body' does not mean that our decayed and diseased bodies will somehow or other be resuscitated so that they may be taken into heaven. What it really implies is that as the spirit of man is expressed through the body here on earth, so in the future state it will express itself with a body appropriate for the other world. 'God giveth it a body as it hath pleased him.'

I think one of the reasons that many people have doubts is because we can't imagine what the hereafter will be like. All we have to do is to try to imagine what it is to be with God. Wild and endless speculation will not get us anywhere. The reality of the resurrection lies not so much in the various 'proofs' of survival, but rather in present everyday experiences. You needn't worry too much therefore as to what happens on the other side. The all-important fact is that Christ will be there and we shall see him face to face. Resist, if you can, the temptation to speculate as to what heaven is going to be like. No one can conceive realistically the nature of the afterlife. We just don't know sufficient about it. We are in God's hands in death as in life, and this is all that matters. Let it be sufficient to be assured that 'eye hath not seen, nor ear heard, neither have entered into the heart of man, the things which God hath prepared for them that love him' (1 Cor. 2.9.). This is all that the Bible tells us about our risen bodies. Perhaps it isn't enough to satisfy our curiosity, but holy Scripture wasn't written to gratify our curiosity.

What will life be like in heaven? It's rather misleading to think of 'going to heaven'. Unfortunately we are prone to think of heaven and hell as places rather than states. We have to rid ourselves of all notions of place, and think rather of conditions. Let's picture heaven rather as coming into complete harmony with God. After all, heaven is where God is, and where God is there is heaven. Heaven can be near to us every day. Heaven is communion with God. Hell is separation from him. We can experience a measure of eternal life now in this present world.

> Lord, give me such a faith as this,
> And then what'er may come,
> I taste even now the hallowed bliss
> Of an eternal home.

Hymns Ancient and Modern, Standard Edition, 278

Eternal life is simply being in fellowship with God. It is not a life which goes on 'for ever and ever'; it is neither endless nor timeless. Rather it is a life of certain quality. Jesus promises us eternal life in the here and now; not simply life after death but fullness of life now in the present. 'I am come that they might have life and that more abundantly.' It is a relationship with God in prayer and in fellowship, in Bible-reading and sacrament—all the essentials we've thought about in our earlier talks.

All the scriptural imagery of heaven—the descriptions of streets of gold, walls of jasper, and gates of pearl— is a merely symbolical attempt to express the heavenly in terms of the earthly. It is to try to express the inexpressible, to explain the inexplicable, so we can rightly discard the white robes and the playing of harps! We have to recognize the obvious limitations of human language. The instrument of language breaks in an attempt to describe the indescribable. Our earthly language is all too limited and inadequate to express the glories of the afterlife. Earthly language, earthly figures, earthly images—all of them seem so incapable of expressing the glories and mysteries of the other world. Although it is only he who knows all the joys and blessedness of heaven, Jesus himself has been comparatively silent about it all. He has given us very little help really in answering the inevitable questions which arise in our minds. He tells us simply that heaven is his Father's home and that in it are many mansions or resting-places—implying a going on from stage to stage in growth and development. 'In my Father's house are many mansions: if it were not so, I would have told you' (John 14.2). The rest is silence. But what a silence! When you think about it it's a silence lit up by one word of assurance—surely the most precious of all his assurances—'If it were not so I would have told you.' Beyond death there is a home waiting for us, where reality shall exceed our fondest dreams; where every provision has been made and every slightest need anticipated. There's a saying about silence being golden, but surely there was never a silence quite as golden as his. I'm sure our Lord's silence is part of his demand for faith. We have to walk by faith and not by sight, and venture everything on our trust in him. After all it's such faith that gives the Christian life its challenge, its adventure, and its zest. The lesson you and I have to learn is one of complete trust in him. Then we shall have no hesitation or uncertainty about the perfect happiness of heaven.

It is our Father's house to which we are going, and that surely is enough. Don't let us be too anxious about precise descriptions, for now we see only through a glass darkly. We know there is nothing to fear, for our dearest hopes will be more than satisfied. If it were not so he would have told us.

We sometimes connect with our picture of heaven the thought of rest from work. I wonder, are we right to think this way? We shall rest but it is not rest as inactivity or idleness. It will be an active rest. 'Rest from weariness, from toil—Yes; rest from work, from service—No!' I'm sure we're not going to spend our time idly plucking harps of gold or wandering aimlessly through paradise, clad in white robes and with crowns on our heads! As I've explained to you, these are only symbols. It is true of course that 'there remaineth a rest for the people of God', but it is the rest of perfected activity and service, of work and worship. To worship in work and to work in worship will surely be part of our gladness in the hereafter. 'His servants shall do him service.' The activities of the heavenly life are beyond are knowledge, but we cannot reasonably doubt that one part of our work will be prayer. Christ is ever interceding for us here on earth; are we going to be debarred from sharing in those same intercessions? I do not think we are. One of our purest joys will be to co-operate with God in his great work of redemption through prayer. When we depart we hope we shall be with Christ; we shall see him face to face; we shall be made like him; we shall be forever with the Lord, and he will be forever with us. Nowhere in the Gospels do we find any warrant that in heaven we shall have nothing to do but 'gaze and gaze on thee', as the hymn puts it. Heaven is a life of perfect fellowship with God, and a sharing in his own work. There will be no idleness or boredom but corporate activity. To live in God's presence will be fullness of joy, for 'we shall be like him because we shall see him as he is'. I don't think we can better the wonderful description of the heavenly life given us by St Augustine: 'There we shall rest, and we shall see; we shall see, and we shall love; we shall love, and we shall praise.'

Will you meet your loved ones again? We can't bear to think of the future life unless we believe we shall be together. God surely would not have given us the gift of love and friendship if at the end he meant to destroy it in death. 'We have loved. We love now. We shall go on loving.' Such a ministry of love and affection commenced on earth will continue in heaven. In the pages of the New Testament reunion is assumed rather than asserted, for the future life is always represented as a society—a state of fellowship. It is described as a 'kingdom', a 'city', a 'community', an 'assembly', a 'home'. How this recognition will be accomplished and brought about as yet we don't fully know, but as Christians we believe we shall all be in one community, one family, knowing each other and praying for each other. This is quaintly but rather wonderfully described in words of John Bunyan: 'There you shall enjoy your friends again that have gone thither before you; and there you shall with joy receive even every one that follows into the holy place after you.' We shall see each other as we really are, with all the blemishes of this present life taken away, for it will surely be a renewal of community and fellowship far more real and perfect than we've ever experienced in this life—a living community of all who belong to Christ in this world and the next. This is what we mean when we repeat the clause in the creed, 'I believe in the communion of saints.'

> One family we dwell in him
> One Church above, beneath,
> Though now divided by the stream,
> The narrow stream of death.
>
> AMR, 272

We are a 'blest communion', a 'fellowship divine', a union of perfect harmony, which death can do nothing to interrupt. We are all 'one in Christ Jesus'. Every time we gather at the Eucharist, that great act of Christian worship which we discussed earlier, we come into this blessed fellowship, where angels and archangels and all the company of heaven join with us in worship and praise, saying:

> Holy, Holy, Lord God of hosts,
> Heaven and earth are full of thy glory.
> Glory be to thee, O Lord most high.

Believing that Christ is waiting on the other side to welcome you—how can you fear to die? God will take you home when he wants you, in his good time. You are tired. Lie back ready to fall asleep in his arms. We are with you are praying for you—'May the Lord in his mercy grant you a holy rest, and peace at the last.'

Comfort from the Scriptures

COURAGE

The Lord is my light and my salvation; whom shall I fear? the Lord is the strength of my life; of whom shall I be afraid?

Ps. 27.1.

These things I have spoken unto you, that in me ye might have peace. In the world ye shall have tribulation: but be of good cheer; I have overcome the world.

John 16.33

If God be for us, who can be against us?

Rom. 8.31

Perfect love casteth out fear.

1 John 4.18

IN ANXIETY

Take no thought for the morrow: for the morrow shall take thought for the things of itself. Sufficient unto the day is the evil thereof.

Matt. 6.34

Martha, Martha, thou art careful and troubled about many things: but one thing is needful: and Mary hath chosen that good part.

Luke 10.41–2

IN PAIN

I reckon that the sufferings of this present time are not worthy to be compared with the glory which shall be revealed in us.

Rom. 8.18

And he said unto me, My grace is sufficient for thee: for my strength is made perfect in weakness. Most gladly therefore will I rather glory in my infirmities, that the power of Christ may rest upon me.

2 Cor. 12.9

FAITH

If ye have faith as a grain of mustard seed, ye shall say unto this mountain, Remove hence to yonder place; and it shall remove; and nothing shall be impossible unto you.

Matt. 17.20

Lord, I believe; help thou mine unbelief.

Mark 9.24

Increase our faith.

Luke 17.5

My Lord and my God.

John 20.28

Your faith should not stand in the wisdom of men, but in the power of God.

1 Cor. 2.5

We walk by faith and not by sight.

2 Cor. 5.7

Now faith is the substance of things hoped for, the evidence of things not seen.

Heb. 11.1

Looking unto Jesus the author and finisher of our faith.

Heb. 12.2

WHEN WORRIED

Take no thought, saying, What shall we eat? or, What shall we drink? ... your heavenly Father knoweth that ye have need of all these things.

Matt. 6.31–2

Be careful for nothing; but in every thing by prayer and

supplication with thanksgiving let your requests be made known unto God.

Phil. 4.6

Casting all your care upon him; for he careth for you.

1 Pet. 5.7

SERENITY

Thou wilt keep him in perfect peace, whose mind is stayed on thee: because he trusteth in thee.

Isa. 26.3

The peace of God, which passeth all understanding, shall keep your hearts and minds through Christ Jesus.

Phil. 4.7

SLEEP

And Jacob awaked out of his sleep, and he said, Surely the Lord is in this place; and I knew it not.

Gen. 28.16

He rebuked the winds and the sea; and there was a great calm.

Matt. 8.26

ACCEPTANCE

The Lord gave, and the Lord hath taken away; blessed be the name of the Lord.

Job. 1.21

I have learned, in whatsoever state I am, therewith to be content.

Phil. 4.11

THANKSGIVING

Offer unto God thanksgiving; and pay thy vows unto the most High.

Ps. 50.14

What hast thou that thou didst not receive?

1 Cor. 4.7

In every thing give thanks.

1 Thess. 5.18

PEACE OF MIND

Be of good cheer; it is I; be not afraid.

Matt. 14.27

Father, into thy hands I commend my spirit.

Luke 23.46

Lord, to whom shall we go? thou hast the words of eternal life.

John 6.68

Behold, I stand at the door, and knock: if any man hear my voice, and open the door, I will come in to him, and will sup with him, and he with me.

Rev. 3.20

HOPE

Behold, there ariseth a little cloud out of the sea, like a man's hand.

1 Kings 18.44

Now the God of hope fill you with all joy and peace in believing, that ye may abound in hope, through the power of the Holy Ghost.

Rom. 15.13

Not as though I had already attained, either were already perfect: but I follow after, if that I may apprehend that for which also I am apprehended of Christ Jesus.

Phil. 3.12

Lay hold upon the hope set before us: Which hope we have as an anchor of the soul, both sure and steadfast.

Heb. 6.18–19

REPENTANCE

I say unto you, that likewise joy shall be in heaven over one sinner that repenteth, more than over ninety and nine just persons, which need no repentance.

Luke 15.7

Behold, Lord, the half of my goods I give to the poor; and if I have taken any thing from any man by false accusation, I restore him fourfold.

Luke 19.8

Repent ye therefore ... that your sins may be blotted out.

Acts 3.19

THE SACRAMENTS

(a) HOLY COMMUNION

As they were eating, Jesus took bread, and blessed it, and brake it, and gave it to the disciples, and said, Take, eat; this is my body.

Matt. 26.26

And he took the cup, and gave thanks, and gave it to them, saying, Drink ye all of it; for this is my blood of the new testament, which is shed for many for the remission of sins.

Matt. 26.27–8

He was known of them in breaking of bread.

Luke 24.35

He that eateth my flesh, and drinketh my blood, dwelleth in me, and I in him.

John 6.56

For as often as ye eat this bread, and drink this cup, ye do show the Lord's death till he come.

1 Cor. 11.26

(b) CONFESSION

Forgive us our debts, as we forgive our debtors.

Matt. 6.12

If ye forgive not men their trespasses, neither will your Father forgive your trespasses.

Matt. 6.15

How oft shall my brother sin against me, and I forgive him? till seven times? Jesus saith unto him, I say not unto thee, Until seven times: but, Until seventy times seven.

Matt. 18.21–2

When ye stand praying, forgive, if ye have ought against any: that your Father also which is in heaven may forgive you your trespasses.

Mark 11.25

To whom little is forgiven, the same loveth little.

Luke 7.47

I will arise and go to my father, and will say unto him, Father, I have sinned against heaven, and before thee, and am no more worthy to be called thy son.

Luke 15.18–19

Let us eat and be merry: For this my son was dead, and is alive again; he was lost, and is found.

Luke 15.23–4

(c) ANOINTING

And they went out ... and anointed with oil many that were sick, and healed them.

Mark 6.12–13

Is any sick among you? let him call for the elders of the church; and let them pray over him, anointing him with oil in the name of the Lord.

James 5.14

The eternal God is thy refuge, and underneath are the everlasting arms.

Deut. 33.27

Yea, though I walk through the valley of the shadow of death, I will fear no evil; for thou art with me.

Ps. 23.4

Lord, now lettest thou thy servant depart in peace, according to thy word.

Luke 2.29

Whom have I in heaven but thee? and there is none upon earth that I desire beside thee.

Ps. 73.25

Who shall separate us from the love of Christ? . . . neither death, nor life . . . nor things present, nor things to come . . . shall be able to separate us from the love of God, which is in Christ Jesus.

Rom. 8.35, 38, 39

For whether we live, we live unto the Lord; and whether we die, we die unto the Lord: whether we live therefore, or die, we are the Lord's.

Rom. 14.8

Eye hath not seen, nor ear heard, neither have entered into the heart of man, the things which God hath prepared for them that love him.

1 Cor. 2.9

The last enemy that shall be destroyed is death.

1 Cor. 15.26

O death where is thy sting? O grave, where is thy victory?

1 Cor. 15.55

Fight the good fight of faith, lay hold on eternal life.

1 Tim. 6.12

Now they desire a better country, that is, an heavenly.

Heb. 11.16

He also himself likewise took part of the same; that through death he might destroy him that had the power of death ... and deliver them who through fear of death were all their lifetime subject to bondage.

Heb. 2.14–15

IMMORTALITY

I know that my redeemer liveth.

Job 19.25

To-day shalt thou be with me in paradise.

Luke 23.43

I am the resurrection, and the life: he that believeth in me, though he were dead, yet shall he live: And whosoever liveth and believeth in me shall never die. Believest thou this?

John 11.25–6

Why should it be thought a thing incredible with you, that God should raise the dead?

Acts 26.8

If in this life only we have hope in Christ, we are of all men most miserable.

1 Cor. 15.19

Behold, I show you a mystery; We shall not all sleep, but we shall all be changed, In a moment, in the twinkling of an eye, at the last trump; for the trumpet shall sound, and the dead shall be raised incorruptible, and we shall be changed.

1 Cor. 15.51-2

For this corruptible must put on incorruption, and this mortal must put on immortality.

1 Cor. 15.53

For we know that if our earthly house of this tabernacle were dissolved, we have a building of God, an house not made with hands, eternal in the heavens.

2 Cor. 5.1

For here have we no continuing city, but we seek one to
come.

Heb. 13.14

Be thou faithful unto death, and I will give thee a crown
of life.

Rev. 2.10

They shall hunger no more, neither thirst any more; neither
shall the sun light on them, nor any heat. For the Lamb
which is in the midst of the throne shall feed them, and
lead them unto living fountains of waters: and God shall
wipe away all tears from their eyes.

Rev. 7.16–7

I heard a voice from heaven saying unto me, Write, Blessed
are the dead which die in the Lord from henceforth: Yea,
saith the Spirit, that they may rest from their labours; and
their works do follow them.

Rev. 14.13

And God shall wipe away all tears from their eyes; and
there shall be no more death, neither sorrow, nor crying,
neither shall there be any more pain: for the former things
are passed away.

Rev. 21.4

Helpful Thoughts

Death is the supreme festival on the road to freedom.
Dietrich Bonhoeffer

Do not seek death. Death will find you. But seek the road which makes death a fulfilment.
Dag Hammarskjöld

To live in hearts we love is not to die.
Thomas Campbell

Dying is as natural as living.
Thomas Fuller

They that love beyond the world cannot be separated by it. Death is but a crossing the world, as friends do the seas; they live in one another still.
William Penn

Grant that I may make my last hour my finest hour.
Old English Prayer

So he passed over and all the trumpets sounded for him on the other side.
John Bunyan

I do not pray for a lighter load, but for a stronger back.
Phillips Brooks

But all shall be well, and all shall be well, and all manner of things shall be well.
Mother Julian of Norwich

A God on the cross! That is all my theology.
Jean Lacordaire

The best prayers have often more groans than words.
John Bunyan

I have never seen what to me seemed an atom of proof that there is a future life. And yet—I am strongly inclined to expect one.

Mark Twain

The best of all is this—God is with us.

John Wesley

Here in this world He bid us come, there in the next He shall bid us welcome.

John Donne

All the way to heaven is heaven.

Catherine of Siena

We thank thee ... for the means of grace and for the hope of glory.

Book of Common Prayer

There is a land of the living and a land of the dead, and the bridge is love, the only survival, the only meaning.

Thornton Wilder

Always be sure of one fact, that Death is a servant, having a Master over him.

Stephen Paget

The gardener asked, 'Who plucked the flower?' The Master said, 'I plucked it for thyself', and the gardener held his peace.

Anon.

I came from God, and I am going back to God, and I won't have any gaps of death in the middle of my life.

George MacDonald

Death—'the ending of our state of pilgrimage and the place of our fully personal encounter with it'.

Ladislaus Boros

Don't worry about me because my bags are packed. I'm ready to go.

Pope John XXIII

Love is not changed by death
and nothing is lost
and all in the end is Harvest.

Edith Sitwell

In the last analysis it is our conception of death which
decides our answers to all the questions that life puts to
us.

Dag Hammarskjöld

We must overcome death by finding God in it.

Teilhard de Chardin

Husband and wife will be in eternity as two hands uplifted
in unending adoration.

Charles Péguy

Readings

Never forget that you are not alone. The Divine is with you, helping and guiding. He is the companion who never fails, the friend whose love comforts and strengthens. Have faith and He will do everything for you.

Sri Aurobindo

Death, the only immortal who treats us all alike, whose pity and whose peace and whose refuge are for all—the soiled and the pure, the rich and the poor, the loved and the unloved.

Last words of Mark Twain

There will come a time when my links with earth will grow weaker, when my powers fail, when I must bid farewell to dear ones still rooted in this life with their tasks to fulfil and their loved ones to care for, when I must detach myself from the loveliest things and begin the lonely journey. Then I shall hear the voice of my beloved Christ, saying 'It is I, be not afraid.' So with my hand in his, from the dark valley I shall see the shining City of God and climb with quiet trusting steps and be met by the Father of souls and clasped in the everlasting arms.

George Appleton *Journey for a Soul*

I know well there is no comfort for this pain of parting: the wound always remains, but one learns to bear the pain, and learns to thank God for what he gave, for the beautiful memories of the past, and the yet more beautiful hope for the future.

Max Muller *Life and Letters*

The secret of how Jesus sets men free through death and resurrection cannot be grasped and set down in words. It is the experience of being grasped when words fail, and all we can do is to point again to the story and expose ourselves to the experience.

Stephen Verney *Into the New Age*

You are anxious about whether you will rise from the dead
or not, but you rose from the dead when you were born and
you didn't notice it ... There is nothing to fear. There is
no such thing as death.

Boris Pasternak *Doctor Zhivago*

Lord, as my mortal hours run by, help me to die to the
flesh, die to myself, die to all that is not of thy
Spirit, die daily. So that I make the last surrender of this
life, not to death, but to God.

Give my soul hunger for its re-making by its Beloved, in
light: and bring me to the finishing of faith, to my own
Easter Day, in thee.

Eric Milner-White in *Journey for a Soul*

There is nothing in the world of which I feel so certain.
I have no idea what it will be like, and I am glad that I
have not, as I am sure it would be wrong. I do not want it
for myself as a mere continuance, but I want it for my
understanding of life. And moreover, 'God is love' appears
to me nonsense in view of the world He has made, if
there is no other.

William Temple in *A Book of Comfort*, Elizabeth Goudge

I have got my leave. Bid me farewell, my brothers! I bow
to you all and take my departure.

Here I give back the keys of my door—and I give up all
claims to my house. I only ask for last kind words from
you.

We were neighbours for so long, but I received more than
I could give. Now the day has dawned and the lamp that
lit my dark corner is out. A summons has come and I am
ready for my journey.

Rabindranath Tagore in *A Book of Comfort*

Pain is terrible, but surely you need not have fear as
well? Can you not see death as the friend and deliverer?
It means stripping off that body which is tormenting you:
like taking off a hairshirt or getting out of a dungeon. What

is there to be afraid of? ... Remember, tho' we struggle against things because we are afraid of them, it is often the other way round—we get afraid *because* we struggle. Are you struggling, resisting? Don't you think Our Lord says to you 'Peace, child, peace. Relax. Let go. Underneath are the everlasting arms. Let go, I will catch you. Do you trust me so little?'

Of course this may not be the end. Then make it a good rehearsal.

C.S. Lewis *Letters to an American Lady*

He smiled up at me trustingly. Then, very softly, he said, 'I'm going to die, aren't I?'

I cleared my throat, searching for words. 'That's a possibility we all have to face. I've faced it—so have a lot of others.'

'I know,' the boy nodded. 'That's why I like to talk to you. You've been through it. You understand.' ...

I had brought my bible with me. I opened its torn pages and in the dim light of the hut I began to read those words that had comforted countless souls before him: 'Yea, though I walk through the valley of the shadow of death, I will fear no evil; for thou art with me; thy rod and thy staff they comfort me'.

I looked over at him. He was lying quietly. I turned to another passage: 'I am the resurrection and the life; he that believeth in me, though he were dead, yet shall he live. And whosoever liveth, and believeth in me shall never die. Believest thou this?'

I put the bible down. His grey eyes were far away and he was listening within himself—to the message those words had brought. After a bit he turned his gaze to mine and said with perfect calm, 'Everything is going to be all right.'

'Yes', I nodded. 'Everything is going to be all right.'

Ernest Gordon *Miracle on the River Kwai*

The truest end of life, is to know that life never ends.

He that makes this his care, will find it his crown at last.
And he that lives to live ever, never fears dying,
Nor can the means be terrible to him that heartily believes
   the end.
For though Death be a dark passage, it leads to
Immortality, and that's recompense enough for
Suffering of it.
And yet faith lights us even through the grave, being
Evidence of things not seen.
And this is the Comfort of the Good, that the grave
   cannot hold them, and that they live as soon as they die.
For Death is no more than a turning of us over from time
   to eternity.
Death then, being the way and condition of life,
We cannot love to live, if we cannot bear to die.

William Penn *Some Fruits of Solitude*

When I go into the next world I shall not feel a stranger.
As a child taken from the left breast cries only to find consolation in the right breast, so shall it be when we pass
from life to death, from life to life ... I always had faith.
Now I have knowledge.

Charles Reid *Malcolm Sargent. A Biography*

We do feel sometimes as if we are left to ourselves to
struggle with it all. Certainly life is not made soft for
Christians; but it is, in the last resort, safe. Christ
stands over against history and in its darkest and most
dangerous moments we receive a new revelation of his
power.

We can never forecast the path God's energy of rescue
will take. It is never any use saying to him, 'I am getting desperate! Please answer my prayer by the next post
and please send an open cheque'. He will answer but not
necessarily like that ...

This general action of the power of God in life is what
we rather vaguely call providence ... It conditions our
whole career from birth to death just as the invisible lines

of force within a magnetic field condition all the tiny iron filings scattered on it. But now and then it does emerge on the surface and startles us by its witness to a subtle and ceaseless power and love working within the web of events. I am sure we ought to think of this far more than we do.

Evelyn Underhill *The School of Charity*

Sometimes when I am far from home and beginning a return journey, the way seems long, the night dark and my body weary. With sudden anxiety I wonder whether I have forgotten my key. Then I remember it does not really matter. When the last mile is ended, and I reach the outer gate, some one who has been waiting and listening will know. As I go up those few steps to the door, locked and un-inviting—suddenly the door will be opened *from the inside*, for some one who waits, cares. I shall cross the threshold into the light and happiness of home. If God be Father will He do less? Why need I fear the locked door or the darkness without? Death has no dominion over Love. That last door will be opened from the inside.

Leslie F. Church *Yonder: A Little Book for the Bereaved*

Then, said he, I am going to my fathers; and though with great difficulty I am got thither, yet now I do not repent me of all the trouble I have been at to arrive where I am. My Sword, I give to him that shall succeed me in my pilgrimage; and my Courage and Skill, to him that can get it. My Marks and Scars I carry with me, to be a witness for me, that I have fought His battles who now will be my Rewarder.

When the day that he must go hence was come, many accompanied him to the Riverside, into which, as he went, he said, Death, where is thy sting? And as he went down deeper he said, Grave, where is thy victory? And so he passed over, and the Trumpets sounded for him on the other side.

John Bunyan *Pilgrim's Progress*